Single Parents
Can Be Proud Parents

To: Freddi

Blessings and love
to you always.

Juanita PsAlm 37:4

Single Parents
Can Be Proud Parents

My Story to His Glory

Dr. Juanita Shaw

Library of Congress Control Number: 2019906404
ISBN: Hardcover   978-1-7960-3715-9
               Softcover   978-1-7960-3714-2
               eBook   978-1-7960-3713-5

-Scripture quotations marked KJV are from the Holy Bible, King James Version (Authorized Version). First published in 1611. Quoted from the KJV Classic Reference Bible, Copyright © 1983 by The Zondervan Corporation.

-THE HOLY BIBLE, NEW INTERNATIONAL VERSION®, NIV® Copyright © 1973, 1978, 1984, 2011 by Biblica, Inc.® Used by permission. All rights reserved worldwide.

Author's exterior Photo by: joroproductions

Print information available on the last page.

Rev. date: 04/28/2020

To order additional copies of this book, contact:
Xlibris
1-888-795-4274
www.Xlibris.com
Orders@Xlibris.com
780760

CONTENTS

A Word From The Author

You never know where life will lead you. Becoming a single parent was the last thing that I imagined when it came to my family. I always dreamed and thought that one day I would get married, have lots of children, and live happily ever after. Unfortunately, it did not happen that way, at least not entirely. I became a single parent when my youngest daughter of four children was five years old. The other children were six, eight, and ten years old. This began a new chapter in my life, and my journey as a single parent began.

Fortunately, I was saved and a Christian, and I was blessed by God to have faith and enough of His Word in me to sustain me at this time. It taught me to trust Him to help me because I knew there would be many challenges in the days ahead. At that time, I was working for an organization that supported many single parents with dependent children. I listened compassionately to many of their stories and some of the things that they faced as single parents, never imagining that one day I also would be sharing my story as a single parent.

Trust in the LORD with all thine heart,
and lean not unto thine own understanding.
In all thy ways acknowledge him,
and he shall direct thy paths.
—Proverbs 3:5-6

Indeed, this is what I did. I trusted God and prayed for His leading and wisdom. I knew that I could never raise my children alone without His help. I can truly say today that it was nothing but His grace and His mercy that guided me victoriously through this whole experience of single parenting. All glory belongs to Him!

Single Parents Can Be Proud Parents is *My Story to His Glory.* It certainly is a reality in my life. It can be one in yours too if you put God first in everything. Keep reading and see how God blessed me to be the proud single parent of four, and be encouraged to know that He is here for you too. To God be the glory, honor, and praise! Amen.

Dr. Juanita Shaw

Train up a child in the way he should go:
and when he is old,
he will not depart from it.
—Proverbs 22:6

I dedicate this book to the jewels of my life, inclusive of my four children (Sonya, Corey, Adrienne, and Tracie), my grandchildren, and great-grandchildren. You are my crown and joy, and it is with great humility that I leave this legacy to you. A special dedicatory tribute goes to my deceased mother, Mrs. Inez Thomas-Wright, for instilling in me excellent moral values and principles that I constantly pass on to my children. My mother introduced me to Christ and she was the greatest example of a Christian that I have ever met. Lastly, to all parents who have been entrusted with the ministry of this worthy calling: parenting. May God forever bless you.

Acknowledgements

I thank God—my Lord and Savior, Jesus Christ, most of all, for His lovingkindness and tender mercies, for enabling and inspiring me to complete this book.

A sincere thank you to my four beautiful and loving children: Sonya, Corey, Adrienne, and Tracie for the great joy that you have added to my life. It is an honor to be called your mother, and you have made me a proud parent. My children, `I love you with all of my heart. I am humbly proud to have you write the Foreword to my book, and my heart is deeply touched by your expressions of gratitude and love.'

I am eternally grateful for the love and support of my family and friends who continuously encouraged me and prayed for me and my children during our journey. A very special thanks to my prayer partners and friends, Eula Scott and Kathy Mitchell, who have stood with me in prayer from the beginning to the end. This is true friendship.

My pastor and spiritual leader, Dr. Marcus D. Davidson has given me his blessings for the "GREAT success" of my book. Dr. Davidson, thank you so much for your encouraging words, prayers, and support.

In this book, I have included the single parent's experiences that have enriched the contents of my work. Valarie Paulino, my niece, and Belinda Miller, my friend, thanks for your contributions.

To my publisher, Xlibris, and everyone on my publishing team, thank you for patiently and professionally guiding me in this process.

A special thank you to Rachel Jozen for your support.

Dr. Juanita Shaw

Foreword

By Sonya, eldest daughter

I was raised in a single-parent home. In a perfect world, a male and a female would get married, have children, and raise them together. That's a beautiful thing, and that's how God wants it to be. However, we are not in a perfect world, and in a lot of homes, children are raised by a single parent.

I thank God for His grace, His mercy, His favor, and His understanding. Jeremiah 29:11 says, "For I know the plans I have for you, declares the Lord, plans to prosper you and not to harm you, plans to give you hope and a future" (NIV). God gave me the best mother in the whole world to raise me up—that was His plan for me. God used my mother as a vessel to bring me into the world, and I must say He picked the right vessel for me. A mother's bond with her children is untouchable. The bond starts in the womb, and it has a lot to do with how God created the woman.

It takes a strong God-fearing woman to raise four children who have their own personalities. My mother is a strong, God-fearing woman. I watched her as a child, and I admired her so much. I used to think that my mother was a star, especially when she sang, and I watched how others were touched by her voice. I watched my mother praise and worship God, raise four children, showed and gave us love, work, and go to college. She had so much influence on me. I sat back one day and realized that I have achieved some of the same things that my mother has achieved. I feel that I am like her in so many ways.

My mother made sure we had everything we needed and some of the things we wanted; however, the greatest gift she gave us was God. My mother taught me that God is the key to everything: love, joy, peace, wisdom, knowledge, success, and so much more. My mother taught me to be a woman of many trades and a master of some. She said to me a couple of times to always have backup plans because life is unpredictable.

She raised her children up in church. She used to let us go out with our friends; however, on Sunday morning, we'd better get up with some excitement about going to church. I think we went to every gospel concert that there was in Miami, Fort Lauderdale, Hollywood—wherever. She would get that money up for us to be in the place if there was a charge, and she would not let anything or anyone stop us from going. We went so much until I said when I got grown, 'I am doing my own thing.' And I did, but the Bible says in Proverbs 22:6, "Train up a child in the way he should go, and when he is old, he will not depart from it," and my mother did that.

My mother also disciplined me when I needed it, and I thank her for it. As a child, I did not like some of her discipline because I wanted my way. Hebrews 12:11 says, "Now no chastening for the present seemeth to be joyous, but grievous, nevertheless afterward it yieldeth a peaceable fruit of righteousness unto them which are exercised thereby." Now I know as a child that it was nothing but love.

Sometimes I wish she was harder on me, and I wish I would have listened to her more. That would have stopped me from making some of the mistakes that I have made in life.

Who she is has a lot to do with who I am. The love she gave her four children is unconditional love. She always can make me see good in a bad situation. She is my best friend, and I love her so much. God gave me a great gift when He gave me my mother. If God were to ask me to come to His kingdom so my mother can stay on earth to do some more of His work, I would say yes to Him because I know in my heart my mother is a virtuous woman (Proverbs 31:10–31).

Congratulations to you, Mom, on your book. I pray it will be a blessing and an inspiration to everyone who reads it.

I love you, Mom.

Foreword

By Corey, only son

It is an honor and a privilege to be able to write a foreword to the new book of my mom, Dr. Juanita Shaw. I believe that my three sisters and I were witnesses to bear firsthand the anointing, the power, and the strength of a single woman raising her four children after the effects of divorce. Even after the divorce, she was determined to make sure that her four children were successful and had the opportunities to be successful. I would like to share with you some important points that were then, and still are, evident of the essential characteristics that granted my mom success as she operated in the office of a single parent.

The first essential quality my mom had that helped her navigate through life as a single mother was that she operated according to the Word of God. She trusted God to lead her, guide her, instruct her, and provide for her. The knowledge and intellect she discovered and developed was born out of her relationship with God. She knew then, and still knows today, that all wisdom comes from God. As a single parent, she had to depend heavily on the wisdom of God to ensure that she not only was a good parent to her children, but she also made sure that she positioned each one of us for success. Mom knew that every decision she made concerning her children would be important concerning the rest of our lives.

The second essential quality that allowed my mom to operate on different levels in life and within different groups and organizations was that she operated according to the principle of love. She loves God very much, to the degree that everything she does, she allows love to be the driving force or motivation that helps her deal tastefully with all mankind. She does not have a negative bone in her body but rather a prevailing spirit of love. Mom loves her four children as well as her grandchildren and her great-grandchildren. There is nothing she would not do to aid, assist, or help any one of her children because she knows that her children will encounter tests and situations in which they would need guidance and assistance in finding the best possible solution. Through love, she gave each of us a secret formula to winning in this world: by loving one another and loving all people. We were never taught to love over the other but rather to love one and the other.

The third essential quality my mom taught us was to be determined and relentless. Mom, who has several degrees, including a doctorate degree, taught us the value of education. She led by example, and still leads this day by example, because she is forever seeking ways to improve her self-service. Mom believes that education not only gives you an advantage in the marketplace, but also continual learning allows you to stay on the cutting edge in society. As a result, all of us have pursued higher learning, which to this day, affords us advantages in the workplace. This would not have been there had we discounted the lessons surrounding a good education. I can remember when I used to hear my grandmother always tell my mom, "You're always on the go and always in school." This is so true as my mom is a facilitator for the Jacksonville Theological Seminary and the Revelation Message Bible College, as well as a volunteer in several community organizations.

The fourth essential quality that my mom embedded into all her four children was respect. We were taught that respect was more than one greeting an elder or older person with the correct salutation but that it also applied to one having self-respect. Mom would not, and still does not, tolerate disrespect on any level. As children, we were taught the value of respect, as well as the consequences of disrespect. Mom, as a single parent, would share with my three sisters and me every night the importance of respect to God first, to one another second, and then to other people as well. Respect is intertwined into every area of life, and mom knew that her four children would need this essential quality to be successful in life.

There are many other points, I believe, you could carry away. However, there aren't enough pages to be able to write each specific detail I witnessed firsthand from my mom, who is directly connected to who and what I am today. Invariably, whenever someone asks who is responsible for me being who I am today, the answer is still the same: the Lord and my mom. I can recall when I played football for Morris Brown College, and we had a game in the Bahamas against Bethune Cookman College, now BCU. I had gotten injured in the second quarter and was stretched out on the field. The sun was so bright, and the pain was very excruciating, so I had covered my face with my hands. Then suddenly, I felt someone touch me with their hand and say, "Corey!" I moved my hands, looked up, and said, "Mama!" My mom had made her way out of the stands, onto the field, past security and the referees, and made it to me, injured on the field. She told me she heard my name across the intercom and was determined to see about her child. Yes, my mom was relentless that day, and she still is relentless today.

Definitely, there are many other instances I could share with you, but I would rather you read this book and allow yourself to experience the journey, the process, and the love she has for her children and other single parents. In this book, you will learn that you can trust God, be determined, and raise strong children in the face of oppositions, societal pressures, opinions, or predictions. We were taught to defeat the odds, and we have.

Thank you, Mom, for your love and guidance. Thank you, readers, for your desire to glean and learn from a woman who would not be denied the chance to raise, lead, and train strong leaders. Allow yourself to get to know the author of this book, and allow yourself to take away golden nuggets that will help you if you are a single mother or single father. You will learn that even though you may be single, you are never alone because God is always with you.

Love always

Foreword

By Adrienne, second daughter

I am thankful for this priceless experience to be able to share and write this foreword to my mother's book. My mother, I believe, is an angel sent from God to raise four beautiful young adults, to teach us the true meaning of life and love, and to be there to help us raise our children and grandchildren.

My mother has always been by my side, through the good and the bad, through happy and sad times, supporting me all the way. She has made so many sacrifices for me, and she has always encouraged me to be all that God created me to be. My words and expression of thanks are countless to my mother, and I am so grateful to God for giving me my mother. She is my closest friend, next to God. I can count on her for Godly wisdom and to be truthful about situations that I am faced with, whether I agree with her Godly counsel or not.

My mother is my precious gem from God. She loves me, my siblings, and her family unconditionally. She has never shown favoritism, and she makes everyone in her presence feel special. I can call on her anytime, day and night, and she always makes time for me, even if only to say a cheerful "hello" or to listen to what is going on in my life.

I am grateful to God that my mother introduced me to Him at an early age and for how she taught us scriptures. I still rely on the words that I was taught earlier in life to help carry me through any situation. She seems to have so much courage and strength in the toughest of times, always having encouraging words and directing me to the throne room. That's because she knows that God has the answer to every problem. I'm so glad that she taught me the importance of prayer.

My mother is God-fearing, giving, joyful, kind, loving, an awesome woman of God, and truly she has all the characteristics of a Proverbs 31 woman. I can truly praise her and call her blessed of the Lord. Mama, I pray that your book of what your experiences as a single parent were like will be a blessing and an inspiration to many.

I thank God for you, Mama, and I love you with all my heart. Thank you for loving me and for teaching me how to appreciate life and the true meaning of love. I am who I am because of your love for me.

Foreword

By Tracie, youngest daughter

Loving, inspiring, giving, humble—Mom, the queen of my heart, shines bright like a diamond, always encouraging and receiving many more accolades for being a wonderful person and the great example of how love should really be. You are such a beautiful woman of God who expresses strong truth, passion, and integrity.

As the youngest to three wonderful siblings, my journey of life with you has been nothing less than awesome. Never can I dare look down because with or without you around physically, I surely can instantly think of your strong mental and spiritual influence.

You've taught me to "look to the hills from whence cometh my help," (Psalm 121:1) and that encourages me to move on with a smile spiritually because like always, everything will be all right and is all right. God's love through you has taught me to love in spite of the circumstances and to never give up. Your love is so necessary not only to me but also to the whole wide world, and that's one reason of many why I don't mind sharing your wonderful wisdom.

You've mastered life even as a single mother, so, Mom, I feel that the love that you've shown me, my siblings, and many others will forever live on, not only through me, but also through the fruits of your labor.

I'm proud of you, I applaud you, and I love you!

Train up a child in the way he should go, and
when he is old, he will not depart from it.
—Proverbs 22:6

Introduction

Single parenting is becoming more prevalent in today's society. There are many single parents in the world for various reasons: death, divorce, separation, and by choice. There may be other reasons, but regardless of the causes, the number of single-parent households are increasing every day. "Today 1 in 4 children under the age of 18 — a total of about 17.2 million — are being raised without a father. Of all single-parent families in the U.S., single mothers make up the majority. According to 2017 U.S. Census Bureau, out of about 12 million single parent families with children under 18, more than 80% were headed by single mothers" ("Single Mother Statistics"... https://singlemotherguide.com).

Do you desire to be a proud parent? Well, keep reading this book. In it, I will share with you some of my own life experiences that helped me have successful outcomes and become a proud parent. I am not saying that the way that I raised my children is the best or the only way to do it, but I know for a fact that putting God first worked for me. I am blessed to be a proud parent using the wisdom that God gave me on how to raise my children.

The purpose of this book is to share with single parents, and parents in general, some of the practices that I used as a single parent. I want to encourage you to make one of the greatest investments that you will ever make in your life with no regrets.

That investment is in your children, in their well-being, and in their future. They are our gifts from God, and He will hold us accountable for these precious jewels. I also want to encourage you that in spite of the many challenges that you will face, with God's help, you can be a proud parent. I am a witness!

Today I am tremendously blessed by the Lord for following His leading in raising my children. It is an honor for me to share *Single Parents Can Be Proud Parents - My Story to His Glory.* I pray that you will be blessed and inspired by this reading.

(<u>Suggestion on how to read this book:</u> You can read it through, chapter by chapter, or you can select the section that interests you the most. My primary concern is that you will be inspired.)

Chapter 1

God's Gifts To Me: Four Children

Lo, children are a heritage of the LORD: and
the fruit of the womb is his reward.
—Psalm 127:3

Our children are God's gifts to us. His Word tells us that they are "a heritage of the LORD, and the fruit of the womb…". As parents, it is our responsibility to care for our children and to prepare them for the future. We have to love our children, watch over them, protect them, provide for them, and appreciate these gifts that God has given to us. Their future depends on our Godly parental guidance and nurturing. Next to God, they have to be at the top of our priority list. We definitely need God's help in fulfilling our duties as parents. I realized this early in my single-parenting journey.

God blessed me with four children—four gifts. I am so very grateful to Him for them. There's something very significant about the number 4 to me. It represents solidarity. I knew that I had to provide a stable and peaceful home environment for my four children. The Holy Spirit inspired me that I could only do this with God's help.

Having four to raise at one time was very demanding. There were four to care for; four personalities to deal with; four to clothe, feed, provide shelter for; four to designate chores to equally; four to settle disagreements between; four with different friends; four with various activities to attend at different schools; four to attend to all of their needs: educational, emotional, physical, social, spiritual, and the list goes on. Sometimes it even became overwhelming and pretty hectic in the house as they had their childhood disputes and growing pains.

The younger years were the most challenging, mainly because I had to be concerned about their safety when they were not in my presence. Their safety was very important to me. I had to make arrangements for them before and after school care because my job required that I be to work early before their buses came in the morning. They returned home before I did in the afternoon. While they were on the waiting list to get into Nova, and when they were younger, I usually depended on my mother to make sure they got on and off the bus safely. The bus stop was near my mother's house, and at one point right on the corner from her house. Sometimes my mother would actually walk them to the bus stop in the morning and meet them in the afternoon.

I sincerely believe that it was the anointing of God that was upon my life that helped me raise my four children. Yes, He gave them to me, and He anointed me to raise them. I conducted a workshop at a women's retreat years ago, and much later God revealed to me that He had anointed me for this great responsibility. The foundational scripture was Isaiah 61:1: "The Spirit of the Lord God is upon me, because he has anointed me to" . . . raise my children. When the revelation hit me, it was like a light bulb came on. Even though they were grown and gone, He revealed to me loud and clear that it was the Holy Spirit that had guided me through this whole experience of single parenting. God is still giving me direction now because although they are adults, they still come to me for guidance. I still continually depend on the Holy Spirit to lead me in giving them Godly advice and counsel.

I know my children "are a heritage of the Lord" (Psalm 127:3). Humbly, I bless the Lord and all that is within me for His heritage He has entrusted me with. Who can guide you through the process of being a proud and successful parent? God can. Of all my accomplishments in life, other than receiving the Lord Jesus Christ as my personal Lord and Savior, I consider being able to raise my children with God's help as my greatest success story.

From left to right: Sonya, Corey, Adrienne,
Tracie …Juanita (middle)

Chapter 2

Spare The Rod! Spoil The Child!

He that spareth his rod hateth his son: but he
that loveth him chasteneth him betimes.
Proverbs 13:24

The words "rod" and "chasteneth" in this scripture both imply that some form of discipline must be used in child-rearing. The kind of disciplining and chastening that we use will help our children make right decisions in life. The Book of Proverbs is filled with many Godly practical principles on how to discipline our children. It encourages us to use the necessary means to correct them early in life for their own benefit and for their future. When I was raising my children, I would tell them that discipline was for their own good, and now they understand it well.

While raising my children, I did not read any books, nor had I heard of any to teach me how to be a good single parent. I know there were probably books out there regarding single parenting, but I never even thought to seek out any. This is why I had to trust God totally and lean on Him completely for direction on how to take care of His heritage, my children, whom He had placed in my care.

At one point, I did try using some of the information that I gained from a college course in child psychology regarding child-rearing and disciplining children. This course taught that you were to ignore bad behavior and praise good behavior. I tried this type of discipline for a period, but unfortunately, it did not work for me entirely. One reason it was ineffective for me, I believe, is that my children were no longer young infants or toddlers. Perhaps if I had started earlier when they were younger, I might have had a more successful outcome with this type of discipline.

It was easy for me to praise good behavior, however, it was very difficult for me to ignore bad behavior after a while. I am not discounting this type of discipline, but I will say that it may work better when you start early, while the children are very young. Since that method of disciplining my children was not working for me, I returned to my traditional method, and I called it as I saw it at that moment; I did not "spare the rod," and I did not "spoil the child."

Of course, we must always use sound judgment when disciplining our children. Sometimes it is not wise to address inappropriate behavior at the time that it occurs, depending on the severity of the behavior. We must wait and be wise before we take action because the intensity of heated emotions could cause a hardship on us. We must use Godly wisdom at all times. God requires us to discipline our children with love. At the same time, we must not be afraid or hesitate to lovingly correct them when they need to be disciplined.

Chapter 3

Thank God For A God-Fearing Mother

Her children shall arise up, and call her blessed.
—Proverbs 31:28a

"Like mother, like daughter"—Have you heard that saying before? I thank God that I was blessed and fortunate to have a Spirit-filled, loving mother who led by a shining example and whose life of faith, love, and prayer helped me tremendously. She was not a woman of many words when it came to the verbal subject of raising children, but her actions spoke volumes concerning child-rearing standards. Mother raised my siblings and me to reverence God, to be loving and kind to others, to be respectful, and to treat all people with the highest respect, especially elders and those who had authority over us. She taught us good manners. She was a single parent for a period of time too, due to the death of my father when I was seven years old.

When my children were born, I found myself following some of the same patterns of discipline and child-rearing methods that my mother used to raise us. I was the twelfth of sixteen children. Even though I found myself a little more lenient than my mother, the standards and expectations that I had for my children were high, and I did set rules for my household. Rule no. 1 was taken from the Bible, Joshua 24:15: "As for me and my house, we will serve the Lord." Next to God, I was in charge. Other rules were unwritten, but my children knew them so well.

I highly supervised my children, monitored their involvements, and was very protective of them. Sometimes they would say that I was too protective, and even others would say the same thing. Despite their comments and judgments, I had to be this way because I took my job as a parent seriously. I knew that I would be honoring God because He had entrusted me with His "heritage" and I loved them unconditionally. My mother loved us unconditionally and protected us too.

Even today I find myself sometimes being extremely concerned with what is going on in their lives. One of the greatest things that I have learned is to be an active and effective listener, to listen to their concerns, and to immediately begin to intercede for them—placing these concerns at the foot of the Cross. That relieves me because I know that God is the one who can handle whatever is going on in their lives better than I can. He is the great problem-solver. Hallelujah!

Following my mother's example, I always provided a clean, firm but loving environment for my family. I did not have the house on the hill or the best means of transportation; however, we made the best of what we had, never complaining or murmuring. This is so amazing as I think about it now. Thank God that our good days did outweigh our bad days. I am a firm believer that what matters most to children is not so much material things; they just want to be kept clean, fed, and to feel loved.

The spirit of love and respect resided in my mother's home, and I prayed to God that His love would abide in my home and in our hearts. My mother certainly made me feel loved, and I did my utmost to make all four of my children feel loved. Today, if you would ask them in or out of my presence about the love that God allowed me to give them, their answers would be identical. They will all say and agree that "Mama loves all of us the same." God taught me and I observed and followed my mother's example. My mother introduced me to Christ at an early age, and I did the same to my children. They all acknowledged Jesus Christ as their personal Lord and Savior at a very early age, and they all were baptized. My mother provided the greatest leadership on how to be a loving parent.

Yes, we, my brothers and sisters arose and called her, our mother, blessed because of the legacy of faith and love that she left behind: how to love and trust God, to love and respect others, and to lead by example. I want to leave the same legacy to my children, my grandchildren, great-grandchildren, and every generation to come. Even now, I receive many blessings and thanks from my children for loving them and teaching them the way of righteousness, about God, and how much they appreciate me for disciplining them. Sometimes they say I should have been stricter with them. I give God all the praise!

Chapter 4

Pouring Into Your Children

Train up a child in the way he should go, and
when he is old, he will not depart from it.
—Proverbs 22:6

As parents, the Word of God instructs us to *"Train up a child in the way he should go, and when he is old, he will not depart from it."* The words "train up" (Hebrew, *chanak*, means initiate or discipline, dedicate, train up), and "way" (Hebrew, *derek*, means a road, a course of life or mode of action), have the connotation of discipline. (KJV Old Testament Hebrew Lexicon…Bible Hub - Lexicon). Parents are to discipline their children, direct them in the right path, and teach them moral values when they are young. This proverb encourages us that this good parenting training in childhood will lead to lives of good moral character and integrity in their adulthood.

Sometimes children will stray away from the Godly parental training that they were taught. We have no way of knowing if they will or will not turn from the teachings that we have taught them from God's word. (One of my daughters in her foreword stated that she said when she became an adult, she was going to do her "own thing".) Nevertheless, I strongly believe that even though they might stray away from it, they will not stay away from it. Eventually they will return. I write this from my own experience. If we do our part faithfully and heartily, God will do His part.

We have been called by God to always exhibit good behavior before our children and to instill Godly wisdom in them. We must not leave children on their own to raise themselves. When correction is needed, we must do so because when we chastise them, it really means that we love them. Just as God chastises those that He loves, we do the same with our children. It may not seem like chastening is love, but the Word of God lets us know that this is the right thing to do.

Here are some encouraging proverbs that teach about child-rearing and disciplining a child. Take some time to read and meditate on them:

> Proverbs 13:24 – He that spareth his rod hateth his son: but he that loveth him chasteneth him betimes.

> Proverbs 29:15 – The rod and reproof give wisdom: but a child left to himself bringeth his mother to shame.

> Proverbs 29:17 – Correct thy son, and he shall give thee rest: yea, he shall give delight unto thy soul.

> Proverbs 19:18 – Chasten thy son, while there is hope, and let not thy soul spare for his crying.

> Proverbs 23:13 – Withhold not correction from the child: for if thou beateth him with the rod, he shall not die.

As you can see, the word "rod' was mentioned in three of these verses. It is indicative that the writer of Proverbs is stressing the importance of discipline when it comes to raising our children. I firmly believe in using good disciplinary measures in child-rearing, but not necessarily with a physical stick or a physical rod. When my parents were raising me, they did use a physical object at times (mostly a trimmed limb off of a bush or a belt) to discipline me. The paddle that my principal used at school was a physical tool, but it was designed to paddle in the right place. I remember only two times getting paddled by my school's principal. Today, I do understand that this is not a method that is used; however, there are other ways to attempt to correct inappropriate behavior.

This book of Godly wisdom that gives us wise counsel on child-rearing is definitely a good book to have your children read. I had my children to read this book often when they were growing up. I recently encouraged them and my grandchildren to continue this practice—a chapter a day each month. This book is also a good one for parents to read because it gives great insights on practical living. I still read Proverbs today along with my children and grandchildren.

We should always want our children to be better than we are, to be more successful in life than us. This is one of the reasons that I tried to pour everything that I had into raising my children. I was determined to make statistics out of a lie. It was said that a single parent could not raise children without them leading destructive lives and that children who did not have a father in the home would be victims of crime and poverty. When I heard this, I was destined to reverse that opinion with my experience as a single parent. I would often say, "The devil is a lie, and Jesus is the truth." I confessed God's Word over my children. Even before I came to know God as I know Him today, I have always believed that words are powerful, and what you confess is what you get. Watch what you say! It is true!

Death and life are in the power of the
tongue: and they that love it
shall eat the fruit thereof.
—Proverbs 18:21

For verily I say unto you, That whosoever shall say
unto this mountain, Be thou removed, and be thou
cast into the sea: and shall not doubt in his heart,
but shall believe that those things which he saith
shall come to pass; he shall have whatsoever he
saith. Therefore I say unto you, what things so ever
ye desire, when ye pray, believe that ye receive them,
ye shall have them.
—Mark 11:23–24

You can have what you say! This is why I made positive
confessions over my children. No matter what was going on or
how contrary they were acting at times, I only confessed what I
wanted them to be or what I wanted them to become. I confessed
often that they belong to Jesus, calling their individual names. I
confessed that they were saved, sanctified, and filled with the Holy
Spirit. I confessed that they would be successful children and that
they would be all that God created them to be. I confessed they
were angels, even when they were acting like devils. I still make
confessions over their lives today.

Believe me, raising my children was not always an easy task.
There was peer pressure, emotional and financial pressures, and
all the other negative things that the enemy would try to use to
destroy a family. But, because I believed in the supernatural power
of God to help me, and because I believed in the power of prayer,
and was consistent in my disciplinary measures, it made life a lot
easier and more peaceful.

Through it all, through many challenges and sacrifices, many tears, and much prayer, we made it! I am a witness that He "will never leave you nor forsake you" (Hebrews 13:5c). He was with us all the way, and He is still with us now. So do not hesitate to pour into your children. They are yours. They are God's gifts to you. There is a purpose for them being born. Hold your head up high and look "to the hills from whence cometh your help" (Psalm 121:1), and make an open confession that you can make it with God's help. Believe that He won't put more on you than you can bear (1 Corinthians 10:13). Thank God for your gifts—your children.

Chapter 5

Raising Children God's Way

Only take heed to thyself, and keep thy soul diligently,
lest thou forget the things which thine eyes have seen,
and lest they depart from thy heart all the days of thy
life: but teach thy sons, and thy sons' sons.
—Deuteronomy 4:9

God holds us responsible for raising our children the right way—
His way. We are to chasten them when they fail to obey. Our
children cannot be expected to be what they have not been taught
to be, or to do what they have not been taught to do.

Parents must take time to do what is necessary to "train up"
(Proverbs 22:6) their children in the way of righteousness. We
cannot leave this obligation to society and the world. I know we
have busy schedules and a lot going on in our lives; however,
providing children with moral and spiritual health in this day and
time is urgent. There are 24 hours in a day, and surely some of that
time can be dedicated to their spiritual growth.

One day while communicating with my son, he told me that he
tithes the 24 hours in a day (a tenth). He said he spends a minimum
of two hours and forty minutes each day in fellowship with the

Father—whether it's reading the Word, praying, meditating, or listening to inspirational music. You may not be able to tithe the time that you spend with your children spiritually every day, but it is important that you do make time for their spiritual health.

Raising children God's way is to raise them according to His Word and about His divine rules and commandments. In doing this, we are teaching them to honor, love, and respect God, themselves, and others. Teach children God's way—to not only know His laws but to follow them. Lead by example. Words are important, but actions say a lot more. Model Godly behavior and Godly standards before them, and expect good fruitful results. Then, they will be able to teach their sons, and their sons' sons... and their daughters and their daughters' daughters. Amen.

Chapter 6

God's Mandate To Parents To Teach Them His Word

*And these words which I command thee this day, shall be
in thine heart. And thou shalt teach them diligently unto
thy children, and shall talk of them when thou sitteth
in thine house, and when thou walketh by the way, and
when thou liest down, and when thou riseth up.*
—Deuteronomy 6:6–7

**The Word of God commands us to teach our children His Word.
My children knew not only the Ten Commandments, but they also
knew many other scriptures. We read the Bible at home as well as
in church. They were involved in church ministries and Sunday
school where they were taught scriptures. At home, I would have
them read some scriptures over and over because as the Word of
God says, "So then faith cometh by hearing and hearing by the
Word of God" (Romans 10:17). As they consistently and repeatedly
read and heard the Word of God, it went into their spirits and it
went to work for them. Today, it is still ruling in their lives and
spirits. I am not saying that they did not stray away from it at times,
but thank God, they did not stay from it. Many times I thought**

they were not listening, but they were, and it is evident in their lives today. To God be the glory!

Every night, and I mean every night, we read something from the Bible, even if it was only one verse. No matter how tired I was or how late it was, we had to do that. After working ten hours a day, later enrolling in college two nights a week, being a full-time mom, we still had our evening devotion every night. No matter what, I knew I had to get some Word in them and in me every day. The Holy Spirit taught me that this was crucial to do so.

They all learned to pray early as children, and each one of them had to lead in prayer individually. It was amazing to hear them pray in their own individual way—to hear the words that would come out of their mouths and from their hearts. Today my heart rejoices when I hear them pray from the heart—all of them are prayer warriors. Sometimes we would pray clockwise in a circle, and everyone knew who would pray next. At other times, we just prayed as we were led by the Holy Spirit. Regardless of the format we used, everyone prayed. I would have them read Psalms at night, especially Psalms 37 and 54. Psalm 37 has forty verses, and I would have them read ten verses each. They still remember this, and sometimes we laugh when we talk about the good old days, sitting most of the time on the floor in the living room with our Bibles, reading and praying together, sometimes all of us falling asleep on the floor. They had their own Bibles and I had their names engraved on them.

Today my children still talk about the scriptures that they used to read together at night. I remember Tracie, after becoming a working adult, calling me one day while sitting in her car during her lunch break. She said, "Mama, I really understand what Psalm 37 means now." I smiled and thanked God. It was in her spirit—the Holy Spirit brought it back to her remembrance at a time when she needed it. As I said before, they were listening, and the Word was taking root in their spirits. So keep feeding your children the Word. Keep feeding them positive truths about themselves, about God, and about others because transformation is taking place. You are planting good seeds, and eventually, they will bring forth good fruit.

One of my daily confessions over my children, grandchildren, and great-grandchildren, is found in Isaiah 54:13, which says, "All thy children shall be taught of the Lord, and great shall be the peace of thy children." I make it a personal confession that applies to them, inserting their names in the scripture. Where it says "thy", I say "my". I believe that when children are taught of the Lord, the result will be great peace. The earlier you do this, the better off they will be. Teach them the Word and teach them to confess the Word over their own lives. I still make sure they get some Word in them daily by sending them scriptures and encouraging words.

Chapter 7

Teaching The Importance Of Obedience

Children, obey your parents in the Lord: for this is right.
Honor thy father and thy mother, which is the first
commandment with promise. That it may be well with
thee, and that thy mayest live long upon the earth.
—Ephesians 6:1–3

My children were taught early the importance of obedience in order to have a long and satisfied life. They were taught to obey God's Word, to obey their parents, and to obey those who had Godly authority over them, as long as they were being told to do the right thing.

They were taught scriptures about obedience from the Word of God. Two of the main scriptures were found in Exodus 20:12 (Ten Commandments): "Honor your father and your mother that your days may be long in the land which the Lord thy God giveth thee.."; and, Ephesians 6:1: "Children, obey your parents in the Lord: for this is right..."

I drove these scriptures home to them every chance I got, and as often as I needed to. Whenever they became disorderly or disobedient, I reminded them of how God felt about it and how I

felt about it, without hesitation. I even posted scriptures all over the house on doors and wherever they had to enter to remind them of what God said and how God and I wanted them to behave and obey.

When they disobeyed or misbehaved, I would often ask them to read Ephesians 6:1–3. Sometimes I would ask them to write what it means to them on paper. I did this for more than one reason. I wanted them to hear what God said—that it would confirm what I was saying; and, this was a good way to check their reading and writing skills as well. Like I used to hear the old folks say, "There's more than one way to skin a cat."

I took advantage of every opportunity to help them make a positive out of a negative situation, while at the same time helping them to improve themselves in other areas. They would have to write out some correct behavioral sentences fifty to a hundred times. I figured if they wrote it enough, it would resonate in their spirits, and they would not make that same mistake again. It helped them not to repeat the same improper behavior. I wanted them to know the importance of obedience and to know that obedience brings blessings.

Chapter 8

Surviving Through Disaster In Faith

When thou passeth through the waters, I will be with
thee, and through the rivers, they shall not overflow thee:
when thou walketh through the fire, thou shalt not be
burned: neither shall the flames kindle upon thee.
—Isaiah 43:2

When my children were young, a major catastrophe happened to us. Our house burned down, and everything we had was destroyed, including those things of sentimental value, such as a library of books, family photo albums, trophies, and school yearbooks, to name a few. This was a new home built from the ground, and in a matter of minutes, it was destroyed by fire. Thank God it was the house that was destroyed and not our lives. It's so amazing how God spared all of us from the fire.

I worked in Deerfield Beach at the time, north of Fort Lauderdale. Everyone, except Tracie, had left the house for school before the fire. That particular day she was waiting for a family friend, a Nova principal, Mrs. Franklin-Brown, to come by and pick her up for school. Tracie was a student at Nova Blanche Forman Elementary School at the time. It was less than thirty minutes, I heard, after Tracie was picked up that the house went up in flames. Thank God my baby was not harmed!

After this tragedy happened, we were all separated temporarily during the week for months until our home got rebuilt and refurnished. Our immediate family, church family, neighbors, and my coworkers all stepped in and offered helping hands. It was love in action. My children were complimented on their behavior while we were separated. I did not worry about their behavior because I had confidence that they would act the way they had been taught to act. I only received praise on their conduct.

None of us complained or murmured or even questioned God. We were so grateful that we were alive and still had one another. All I remember is that I knew my home needed repairs and I did not have the money for them. I had prayed to God about this matter. When I got the news that my house was on fire, I remembered what I had prayed for, not knowing how the answer would come. I am not saying that God has to always allow a tragedy to happen in our lives to get our attention or to bless us, but I am saying that I did pray for home repairs—just did not know how it was going to happen. Even though it was a long waiting period, the house got repaired, thank God. We never stopped going to church or trusting God during this time, and He preserved us in our crisis. Isaiah 43:2 is so real in our lives. God was with us.

This was strong faith. It was evident that my children had been listening when they were being taught about trusting God in everything, and the Word of God was alive in them. Of course, we were inconvenienced, but the love that was shown to us during this time almost made us forget about what had happened.

God blessed us tremendously: materially, monetarily, and spiritually and with so much more that we really did not think about the old stuff that we had lost. Our faith definitely went to another level. We got new clothes, new shoes, new furniture, and a new roof—more and better. God made a way for us and gave us more than what we had before. It reminds me of the story of Job in the Bible: "Also the Lord gave Job twice as much as he had before" (Job 42:10c).

I am a witness that He is Jehovah-jireh, the Lord who provides. He is Jehovah-shalom, the God of peace. He blessed us inwardly with calm and peace, and He touched the hearts of the people to be there for us outwardly to do what they could to help us. The love that we received from others was immeasurable! Praise God!

Surely God will be with us through every situation, test, trial, and temptation. He will safely carry us through, if we only trust Him to do it. All we have to do is to stay focused and keep our eyes on the "prize"—Christ Jesus—and be determined that we will let nothing "separate us from the love of God, which is in Christ Jesus our Lord" (Romans 8:39de).

Chapter 9

The Child's Total Well-Being

And the very God of peace sanctify you wholly; and I pray
God your whole spirit and soul and body be preserved
blameless until the coming of our Lord Jesus Christ.
—1Thessalonians 5:23

My children's educational, emotional, mental, social, spiritual, and
physical growth and health were extremely important to me. Man
is a "triune being"—body, soul, and spirit—and I was taught early
in life that every part must be satisfied to have a balanced life. As
a result, I tried with all I knew to see that these needs were met in
my children's lives. I constantly sought God for wisdom, and God
taught me how to fulfill these needs to the best of my ability. The
Word of God instructed me to "Ask, and it shall be given unto
you" (Matthew 7:7), and this is what I did for many answers to
our needs. I asked for wisdom often (James 1:5).

Glory be to God! I did my best to make sure my children
were fed properly. I was able to stretch the dollar wisely so that
they could have balanced meals. I did not get food stamps or
any subsidies from the government, but they were always fed and
clothed properly. I did not worry about getting name brands, and
they didn't either. We used Zayre's, J. C. Penney's, and Sears a lot

to get their school clothing and shoes. I knew how to sew, so I made some of their clothes.

My children were able to live in a state of serenity, not having to worry about where they would live or what they would eat or wear. This is when I really learned the meaning of budgeting. I knew what I had to work with, and I did not plan for anything outside of that or overextend myself, providing only their essentials.

Communication is of utmost importance in raising children. I took time to communicate with my children. No matter how exhausted I was, I extended myself to find out what was going on in their heads, as much as I could, even if I had to pry it out of one of the other siblings. We talked about everything, including drugs, relationships, sex, about what was going on in school and in the neighborhood. Of course, I know they had secrets, as I found out later when they were grown. However, at that time, our conversations were pretty open, and I tried to stay on top of everything the best that I could. All I could do was all I could do.

We went to Sunday school and church together on a regular basis—every Sunday unless someone was sick. I never sent them. I always took them and stayed with them. We worshipped God together. I knew how they behaved in church because I was there. They knew the house of God would be respected at all times, and they knew I was watching their conduct. Tracie reminded me that I pinched her a few times when she was doing something disorderly.

My children participated in leading worship, and they sang, prayed, and read scriptures aloud in church. As a whole, they participated in church functions and activities that promoted their spiritual growth. By attending to their spiritual, emotional, and spiritual needs to the best of my knowledge, I believe this gave them balance. My children seemed to enjoy a happy childhood, and that was most important to me.

When they were in their early childhood education years, and they were being promoted to the next grade level, I would go to the ABC School Supply Store and buy books on reading and math for the upcoming school year. This was done so they would have a head start in the next grade. During the summer, before they went to spend time with their great-grandmother in Georgia and after they returned, we would spend a portion of their time studying these books.

When I think about it now, I try to remember how I was financially able to do this for my children. Knowing that their future was at stake, and they were in a very competitive school environment, I wanted them to feel confident and to be successful. I willingly made whatever sacrifices were necessary for them without regret. I put my needs on hold a lot of times for them.

Chapter 10

Their Education Was Vitally Important To Me

He maketh me to lie down in green pastures.
—Psalm 23:2a

Monitoring their educational needs was a tedious task at times. I remember having to check their homework every night, having them read something from the Bible, from the newspaper, or a book of some sort and then write me a paragraph about what they had read. I would grade the paper as if I was their teacher in school. Yes, we do send our children to school for teachers to teach them, but I was a firm believer that I was their first teacher. I had to help them as much as I could at home. If you talk to my children apart from me, they will confirm everything that I am writing, and they probably have more to add to this because their memories are probably sharper than mine.

All of my children attended the Nova Schools Complex—from elementary through high school. All of them graduated from Nova, except one who finished her last year at Piper High School. Nova is a very prestigious school. I placed my children's names on the long waiting list immediately when I heard about Nova, before they entered elementary and middle school. Tracie's name was placed on the waiting list immediately after she was born. I wanted my children to be a part of what I believed was an exceptional educational program. It also attributed to my children being exposed to different ethnic groups and races. I find that very beneficial today, as my children are able to get along with and relate to others in a diverse society.

At one point, all of us were in school as I was attending a couple of classes once a week at a local junior college, working on my first degree. I think one of the reasons I originally went to college was to pave the way for them and to be able to help them with their studies in school as well as to help them prepare for college. I ordered a whole library of books on different colleges, financial aid, what foundations gave grants, even years before they reached high school. I studied these books carefully in an effort to be prepared for what was to come after their graduation from high school.

Preparing the way for them, I believed, was a part of my job as a parent. I wanted to help prepare them for college—to be able to help enhance their reading and writing skills that they would need for college. I knew these were essential tools they would need in their future studies. They are all excellent content writers and very good verbal communicators today.

From left to right: Adrienne, Sonya, Corey,
Juanita, Tracie (Teenagers)

Chapter 11

Making The Necessary Sacrifices

And whatsoever ye do in word or deed, do all in the name of
the Lord Jesus, giving thanks to God and the Father by him.
—Colossians 3:17

I learned early to do everything that I was doing for my children, to do it with all my heart as if I were doing it for Jesus Himself. Yes, I made so many sacrifices with God's help to become a proud parent. I remember when my son went off to college in 1988; he left home with a suitcase and a Bible. He was just as content as he could be. I was too because God assured me that he would be okay. The foundation had been laid, and I trusted God to take care of Him, and God did cover him while he was in college.

I would send my son $150 every month, which was a BIG sacrifice at that time. It has always amazed me how I was able to send what was an enormous amount of money at the same time each month. His sisters contributed some too. I got paid once a month and he was included in my budget. God always made it happen. A lot of times it was meant taking my own lunch to work, but it did not matter. I did it, not grudgingly, but happily. My joy was knowing that my child was okay because I was concerned about his well-being. I made these sacrifices so he would not be tempted to get into something that would bring dishonor and shame to himself or his family, and most of all to the Godly principles that he had been taught. His sisters and I, with the help of God, pulled it together for him. Today, we brag about Corey D, and we love him so much that we would make the same sacrifices and more if we had to do it again.

My children were all able to participate in school activities and trips. Adrienne was a part of a thirty-student travel group that traveled all over the United States and even out of the country to Cayman Islands. Tracie was a member of a Nova Chorale group that traveled extensively throughout the United States. Corey was a football player since the ninth grade. Sonya was on the drill team. All these activities required money. Sometimes the school would provide scholarships, but most of the time it required out-of-the-pocket sacrifices on my part. Because I wanted them to have an out-of-the-ordinary worldview, I made whatever sacrifice was necessary to make it happen for them.

When they were younger, there would be times when they would come and say, "Mama, I need $50 . . ." or whatever it was for a trip or a function. I would say, "I don't have it." They would say, "Write a check." I would say, "You have to have money in the bank when you write a check." We laughed, but they were very serious about the matter. I prayed about it. Sacrifices had to be made in most cases, but God always provided.

Everything that you do for your children, and every sacrifice that you make for them, do it out of a pure heart and as if you were doing it for the Lord Himself. You will realize how much lighter your load becomes. Say, "I am doing this for Jesus." It worked for me. I have no regrets for the sacrifices that I made for my children. If I had to start all over again as a single parent, after knowing what I know now, I would have made even more sacrifices.

Chapter 12

Parenting Is A Full-Time Job

I can do all things through Christ which strengtheneth me.
—Philippians 4:13

My children kept me busy. We led very active and busy lives. I was a full-time mom, a full-time worker outside of the home, and a part-time college student at one point. The church and school activities and functions were one thing, but they had other involvements as well. We had family activities also. I used to take them to the zoo in Miami at least once every two weeks—all it cost was gas and snacks. All of them memorized the lineup at the zoo. They had it down pat—first came the snakes, then the monkeys, then the elephants, etc. If they got tired of going there, they never showed it, and they always seemed happy when we went. I also enjoyed it.

Some of their other entertainment included going to the skating rink on Saturday nights. I was singing in a gospel group, and when we did not have a previous function to attend, I would allow them to go skating. This was one of their favorite hangouts because they were able to meet their friends there. So from 8:00 p.m. to 12:00 a.m., when they were older, they were allowed to go without me going with them. I would drop them in front of the door, even though they wanted me to drop them off away from the front entrance. I never could figure this one out, but I think it was because they did not want their friends seeing their mother dropping them off and giving them a hug. I never received a bad report while they were there, and they evidently conducted themselves in a respectable manner. I would always take them and always pick them up at 12:00 a.m. promptly. They were always ready when I came, so I would not have to go inside to get them in front of their friends.

There were school activities. Before they all got accepted into Nova, they were at different schools. I had to attend PTOs and other school functions at their different schools, and I did so faithfully because it was my duty as a parent. I had to let my children know that I was interested in their education and future. It made them feel proud to have their mother meet their teachers and to hear their teachers share their progress in school with me.

In addition, there were church activities. I was director of the youth department for several years. This automatically meant that we all would be attending church regularly and be a part of the youth activities. They all participated in church ministries: Tracie sang in the youth choir, and Sonya, Corey, and Adrienne were members of the youth usher board. They enjoyed participating in these ministries. It is important to get your children involved in some church ministries. Find out what gifts and talents they have and nurture them.

My children attended Sunday school eagerly and faithfully. This was another opportunity for them to be able to socialize with their friends after Sunday school. I remember not having to tell them to get ready for church or Sunday school. Everyone would be going to Sunday school and church unless they were ill. Besides them not complaining about going, they knew that if they missed either for any reason other than for an unforeseen reason, their extracurricular or weekend plans were finished. There would be none! This was, I believe, teaching them how to be consistent and showing them the importance of worship and their relationship with God. They seemed to enjoy attending worship and participating in the church activities.

Looking back, I remember how they used to beat me getting ready for church and would sometimes have to wait for me. Our Sunday school started at nine o'clock in the morning. It was always amazing how we never talked about what we would be wearing, but when they came out of their rooms, we all would be color-coordinated most of the time. The people at church thought we had planned it, but we had not—like-mindedness.

I thank and praise God for giving me the strength to do all of the things that I was able to do with and for my children. Only in the strength of God can we do all things. He is the only one who gives us strength to accomplish all that we endeavor to do. He is the source of our strength and our "portion forever" (Psalm 73:26b) . Amen.

Chapter 13

Teaching Children The Value Of Respect

For as many as are led by the Spirit, they are the sons of God.
—Romans 8:14

As I read, studied, and meditated on the Word of God, the Holy Spirit inspired me on what to do and how to do it when it came to raising my children. I spent time in the Word and prayer, seeking the Holy Spirit's guidance and wisdom when it came to making decisions that would affect my family. When there was a decision to be made, whether it was considered major or minor, I always sought the Holy Spirit's leading. Even with matters some might call small, such as whether they would go to a Saturday night street party. I would pray about my decision, and I would ask questions, such as whose party it is and where it is located, would parents be there and if could I meet the parents, and so forth and so on. After seeking God and getting answers to my questions, I would make a decision as to whether anyone would be going. The same worked for going to movies or spending the night at someone else's house or other activities. It is very important to know who your children are with at all times and that they are supervised at all times. Most important is to rely on the Holy Spirit's guidance.

The Holy Spirit inspired me to teach my children the value of respect. Respect is still a key word in our vocabulary. I am high on respect, and they are too. They were taught to respect all people, no matter how anyone looked, how they smelled, and what they did or did not have. They were taught never to laugh at handicapped or disabled persons; instead, they were taught to have compassion and love for them and to pray for them. One time, when I was teaching my children a lesson on respect and how not to pick at old people, I used the example of the children in the Bible in 2 Kings 2:19-24 that tells how some children mocked an old man, Elisha, and God allowed two she bears to come out of the woods and tare forty-two children. When I told them this story, they became very quiet. The point that I wanted to get across to them is that God does not like ugliness, and that they are to honor and respect elders and others, and not to pick on or belittle anyone because God would not be pleased. Today, I must say that they are very respectful of others.

I constantly reminded my children of their duty to respect God, others and their property, and to respect themselves. Even to one another, they were taught to say "please" and "thank you" when they asked one another to do something for them or asked something of them. In the beginning, this did not come across too good with them, but as my mother used to say, "Practice makes perfect," and "Charity begins at home and spreads abroad." She engraved this in me, and I engraved it in my children. The more they practiced it, the easier it became for them to show love and respect to each other. When they went out, it was easy and habitual for them to show respect toward others.

God requires us to teach our children how to respect and the value of respect. When I look at what is happening in the world today with some of our young ones, and what they are allowed to get away with, my heart is deeply saddened—lack of discipline and lack of respect. What seemingly is a fear that some parents have of their children is also disturbing to me. I am proactive when it comes to children respecting their parents. I have little tolerance for a disrespectful child. Parents must begin to teach the value of respect to their children when they are young.

In addition, while teaching them respect, parents must not be afraid to chastise and discipline their children when it is necessary to do so. After all, "Who's raising who?" is a question I often ponder. I remember when I was a supervisor at a local driver's license office, I was appalled at the way some teenagers were talking to their parents. I would sometimes say, "Who's the parent here?" Would you believe some of the parents would give me a look like, "Don't talk to my child that way!" My flesh would literally crawl when I would hear some of the remarks made by these children to their parents. Unbelievable! I guess the parents were afraid of being embarrassed more or afraid to think about what would happen when they got home, if they reprimanded their children in public. Anyway, there was a change of attitude, at least for the moment; they probably felt that I would not wait on them as long as they were being disrespectful to their parents.

What parents cannot afford to do is to lead their children to believe that they are afraid of them, or that they are afraid to correct them when necessary. Some parents have allowed this to their disadvantage. Inappropriate behavior was not tolerated in my household. Talking back or being sassy (that's what my mother called it) was a no-no. I demanded my children to have and show respect. Yes, they tried me, but it did not work. I remember one day after coming home from a hard day's work, having stopped by the grocery store, I asked them to help put the groceries away. One of them had an attitude and said something that I felt was "smart mouth." At any rate, it was unacceptable behavior. I was tired, but I had to correct that immediately to let them know this was being disrespectful. I also wanted them to know this type of behavior would not be allowed in our home. I picked up a gallon of milk and acted as if I was going to throw it at them, and they all looked at me very strangely. They were shocked to see me act that way, but it got their full attention. No one ever challenged me again in that manner. Sometimes I think they probably laughed at me behind my back and probably said I was weird, but it's okay. I did what I had to do.

One of the greatest principles on love and respect that I taught my children comes directly from the Word of God found in Luke 6:31: "And as ye would that men should do to you, do ye also to them likewise." They were constantly reminded of this one: "Do unto others as you would have them do unto you" (paraphrased), often called the Golden Rule. What we gleaned from this is: You are to do unto others as you would have them do unto you, not as they do unto you. My children were raised on this principle. They are sometimes disturbed today when they witness unkind and disrespectful people. Still, whether others treat us the right way or not, my children were taught to love them and treat them right because this is a command from God.

Overall, I must say so, my children are some of the most respectful children I have ever met. To God be the glory! "Respect" continues to be a large part of their character. When they talk to me about others' impolite behaviors and when others are so disrespectful to them, I encourage them that everyone was not raised like them. They agree, and they are able to move on and lower their expectations of people. Being led by the Holy Spirit allows them to be able to do this.

Chapter 14

Good Manners Are Key

Correct thy son, and he shall give thee rest; yea
he shall give delight unto your soul.
—Proverbs 29:17

My children were raised to have good manners. I wanted them
to know that when they went out into the world, good manners
and good habits would be so customary that it would be a natural
thing for them to do what was right. Another reason I wanted my
children to have good manners and to be respectful to one another
was I wanted them to know that no one outside of our home should
be treated with more love and respect than the ones who lived in
our home. They were taught to be polite and courteous at all times
to all people and to each other. I believe that good manners are the
key to good success.

I taught my children to say "yes, ma'am" and "yes, sir" and
"no, ma'am" and "no, sir" to elders. They were taught to say "yes"
and not "yeah." I remember when we used to go to the grocery
store weekly, and how the people were glad to see my children
with their good manners. When they would say "yes, ma'am"
and "no, ma'am," the people seemed very impressed. Sometimes
they even rewarded my children for their good manners and good

behavior. Teaching my children lessons for life that they would carry throughout their lives was very important to me, and I took advantage of every opportunity to do so. Even today they still say "yes, ma'am" and "no, ma'am," "yes, sir" and "no, sir."

When people look at my children and observe them still exhibiting good manners as a natural habit, and see the fine young man my son has become and the fine young women my daughters have become, they still ask me, "How did you do it?" I tell them that God did it through me. Also, I tell them with a smile, "I instilled the fear of God and the fear of me in them." Even though it sounds jokingly to them, I am very serious about that. I had to do it because at one point, they were all bigger and taller than me.

Teaching your children to have good manners is key. It will take them a long way in life. My mother used to say, "Good manners will take you farther than money." The scripture tells us, "Train up a child in the way he should go, and when he is old, he will not depart from it" (Proverbs 22:6).

Chapter 15

No Help From The Government

But my God shall supply all your need according
to his riches in glory by Christ Jesus.
—Philippians 4:19

Despite the fact that we received no public assistance, we were
blessed to be able to live on what available resources we had—
my meager paycheck and occasional gifts from family members.
Regardless, we always had food to eat. It might not have always
been what we wanted, but we ate. I always tried to prepare my
children balanced and healthy meals daily, especially for breakfast
and dinner because I did not always know what the school lunch
meals consisted of. Even though I did check the lunch menu from
time to time, I had no way of knowing if they actually ate their
lunches.

I did apply for assistance, but the government said I made too
much money to receive food stamps. I could not quite understand
that with the low salary that I received at the time and having
five mouths to feed. According to their eligibility standards,
however, it was true. I know because I worked for the Department
of Public Welfare, later known as the Department of Health and
Rehabilitative Services, for a number of years—the latter years

as an eligibility worker for the Food Stamps Office. I did my own eligibility budget, and no, I was not eligible. We never went hungry, thank God. I knew how to budget my money, and I knew how to stretch the dollar and to stretch the food. I made a weekly menu, and I took my checklist to the grocery store (they went with me) and purchased only what was on the list.

In spite of it all, we managed well. My son was able to get his Jheri curl, and my daughters and I were able to go to the hairdresser every two weeks. Of course, back then, it did not cost much to get your hair washed and hot-comb pressed—something like $3 each every two weeks. We were not doing perms or the weaves then. I do not remember how much Corey's Jheri Curl cost, but he diligently kept it up. He worked part time so he was able to do it. After a while, we (the girls) switched to wearing Afros or Jheri curls to be more economical.

A WAY OUT OF NO WAY! Sometimes I did not know where the money would come from for the school trips or for special school activities and functions, but God would always make a way. I used to hear my mother say "God will make a way out of no way." He certainly did it for us, without any government assistance. Thank God that we did not have to do anything illegal or immoral to survive! Believe me, I did experience firsthand 1 Corinthians 10:13d: "God will make a way of escape." Sometimes when I was down to my last dime, one of my brothers would come by and just hand me $50 or $100. I considered it to be God at work. Through it all, we survived, and He is not through with us yet. I must say that I am proud of these ambitious, hardworking, and loving human beings that God has blessed me with who were very appreciative of what they had.

Along with being involved in their lives while they were growing up, I managed (without government assistance) but with the help of God, to be able to complete my AA degree at Broward

Community College, which allowed me to get a job promotion and provide a little more income for the household. Also, when they all became fourteen years old, they got part-time jobs while in school. The agreement was that their grades must be kept up, and they honored that agreement. At one time, they all worked for the Ponderosa Restaurant and at another time for a marketing firm. As a result, they developed good work ethics, and for that, I am grateful.

BUT GOD! God provided! He took a little and made much out of it. My children always went to school clean and well fed. They were taught at an early age to appreciate what they have and not to look down on themselves because someone else seems to have more. I would constantly remind them of some principles that I was inspired by the Holy Spirit to tell them. I would say: Appreciate what God has blessed you with, and never think you are less than anyone else. Always keep your head up, never look down—always look up. (My son reminds me that he has never forgotten that I told him this years ago, and said he has never looked down again.) Never be jealous or envious of anyone else—of what they have or how they look or where they live. Appreciate who you are and always to be grateful. I had them to read Psalm 121 frequently. They grasped these Holy-Spirit inspired principles then and still live by them today. I did whatever was within my power to keep their self-esteem high and to instill good morals and values in them. I have never heard them complain about any of the above. They continue to express their thankfulness to me regularly for instilling these principles in them.

God's resources are far greater than the government's resources. We are living witnesses today that our "God will supply ALL your need . . ." (Philippians 4:19). He did it for us. He will do it for you, if you believe and place your total trust in Him. God is no respecter of persons (Romans 2:11).

Chapter 16

Taught To Never Be Intimidated By Others

I will praise thee, for I am fearfully and wonderfully made:
marvelous are thy works; and that my soul knoweth right well.
—Psalm 139:14

My children went to school with children who had rich parents and lived in very prominent communities. Since they were taught early to love themselves and to be grateful for what they had, they were never intimidated by others or covetous of others. They even became close friends to many of them. After they were older, my children spent several weekends in Emerald Hills (Hollywood, Florida) with some of their school friends in very nice neighborhoods and homes. They learned to appreciate the better things in life early, and they never showed any signs of jealousy or intimidation. Corey attended many Bar Mitzvahs and Bat Mitzvahs with his Jewish friends. I was always able to come up with the minimum $25 gift for him to take to the affair, though I believe if he had not brought anything, they still would have welcomed him. My children still remain in contact with many of their Nova classmates today. That Nova clan is like family, regardless of the year they graduated from Nova.

I am appreciative that my children were exposed to other cultures and different environments during their early years in school. Nova accounts for a large portion of this, and I also involved my children in community activities and politics with other races when they were young. My children were campaigning early, as well as being involved in several community services. It helped tremendously and they are involved in community services today.

Their classmates and friends did not make them feel inferior. They were able to fit in with ease. My children never made demands on me or complained that I should do more for them or that they should have more because some of their friends had more. Brand name clothing and shoes were never a conversation piece or an issue in our household. They appreciated what I was able to give them, and they received it with gladness and thankfulness.

When they were younger, I used to go to the store and buy their clothes and shoes without them. They would be happy just to get something new. As long as they were clean, fed, sheltered, and assured that they were special and loved, they were content. My children lived Philippians 4:11: "Not that I speak in respect of want: for I have learned, in whatsoever state I am, therewith to be content." To the best of my ability and with the limited resources that I had, I made sure their needs were met. Three times a year, we went shopping for new clothing and shoes: Christmas, Easter, and for the new school term. That was it! At Christmas and Easter, it was only one outfit and one pair of shoes for the church's holiday programs. I made their Easter outfits a few times. They wore them proudly.

My children learned Psalm 139:14 early. We read it, and we confessed it: "I will praise thee: for I am fearfully and wonderfully made: marvelous are thy works: and that my soul knoweth right well." They were told often how special they were to God and to me. They were taught early how to feel good about themselves and how to always be themselves. It is very important to reinforce a child's self-worth to him or her—to instill positive values in your children.

Chapter 17

They Were Not Perfect Children

Chasten thy son while there is hope, and let
not thy soul spare for his crying.
—Proverbs 19:18

No, they were not perfect children. They had their flaws too. They made mistakes. There were many challenges, and they had some mischievous moments. Now that they are adults, they even talk about some of them when we are together, sharing the past and old stories. From time to time, I would hear some things that I would not have approved of. However, I am so thankful to God that no one never came knocking on my door while I was home provoking a fight, and no one ever shot through my doors or windows or flatten my tires because of bad confrontations with my children. For this, I am so grateful because I know times are so different now. This is one of the reasons why having close communication with your children is very important. You will never know everything that they do, but if you spend time with them and communicate with them as much as you can, you will have a pretty good idea of what is going on—a God-given parent's intuition.

As the scripture says, we must "Chasten the son, while there is hope, and let not thy soul spare for his crying." When my children needed chastening, I did it. They were disciplined for whatever inappropriate behavior occurred that I thought needed disciplining. I took away privileges. I gave additional chores. I required more studying and more writing assignments. When they deserved praise, I was the first to give it to them. I chastised and disciplined them because I felt that their future depended on it.

During the time I was raising my children, it was a lot easier to discipline a child without the threat of them calling or involving the law enforcement authorities. I have personally heard a child threaten his parent that he would do this, and the parent looked so afraid and nervous, probably embarrassed and shocked as well. Can you imagine a child whom you are taking care of, whom you are making all kinds of sacrifices for, threaten to call law enforcement on you? Can you imagine living in your own home being afraid of your own children because you chastised them? Unthinkable!

Well, in many instances and in many households it happens a lot. I see parents afraid to discipline their children because of the fear that the parent might be the one being chastised or disciplined by the law. Sad! I remember when I was a child, if we were caught doing wrong, we were disciplined by other adults and our parents as well for one act of disobedience. If our neighbors chastised us, it was okay with our parents. Not so today! Nevertheless, I still believe the old saying that "it takes a village to raise a child."

There are many disciplinary measures that can be used to get the message across to our children to let them know what will or will not be tolerated. We must do whatever it takes within our means that is legal and proper to help our children have a healthy and successful life. Inappropriate behavior must be corrected immediately and with urgency. The key is to start early when they are young. I have always believed that you must get them under control before the age of ten because after that they have a mind of their own. I also believe that if you are consistent with your discipline, there will be less chaos. We must do our very best and trust God for good outcomes.

Yes, we had numerous ups and downs, and my children had their moments, but by the grace of God, we were able to work through them. I bought a wall picture one day that says, "If God brought you to it, He will see you through it" (Author unknown), and this was very encouraging. "Thanks be to God which always causeth us to triumph in Christ . . ." (2 Corinthians 2:14). I owe it all to God who helped me—the Holy Spirit who guided me every step of the way. I can truly say, like the apostle Paul in Philippians 4:13, "I can do all things through Christ who strengtheneth me."

Chapter 18

What Are You Thinking?

With God all things are possible.
Matthew 19:26

I know some of you must be thinking, "How did she do all of this?" Sometimes, when I look back over my life and over our lives, I ask myself the same question. But the answer is easy: GOD. That's the only way I did it. Nothing but His grace and His mercy brought me through this journey of single parenting. For that, I say thank you, Lord, for all You have done, all You are doing, and all that You are going to do for me and my family.

You can do it too! If you are a single parent and thinking and wondering how you are going to make it, just know that with God, all things are possible. Seek His guidance and direction, and trust Him with all your heart. God is true to His promises—He cannot and will not lie. He will put the right people in your path to be a blessing to your life and your children's lives. He'll open doors that need to be opened, that no man can close. He'll close doors that need to be closed, that no man can open. Trust and obey Him!

Whatever you do, don't give up! Rely on the strength and the wisdom of God to see you through. As the word of God says, "... if God be for us, who can be against us?" (Romans 8:31) Believe and know that God's love for you and your loved ones is limitless and powerful. Think BIG!

From left to right: Corey, Tracie, Adrienne, Sonya, Juanita (middle)

Chapter 19

Words Of Encouragement To The Single Parents

Ah Lord God! Behold, thou hast made the heaven
and the earth by thy great power and stretched out
arm, and there is nothing too hard for thee.
—Jeremiah 32:17

You too can be a proud and successful parent. There is nothing too hard for God, and there is nothing He cannot accomplish through you. His Word is full of encouragement for parents. Some of my inspirational ALL scriptures that I meditated on a lot during my journey were: Matthew 6:33, it says, "Seek ye first the kingdom of God and his righteousness, and ALL these things will be added unto you." Another one that I treasured is found in Philippians 4:13: "I can do ALL things through Christ who strengtheneth me"—ALL things! In Romans 8:28, Paul writes, "And we know that ALL things work together for good to them that love the Lord, and to those who are the called according to his purpose"—ALL things! These scriptures encouraged me that God had it ALL in His hands.

When we seek God first and seek His righteousness first, there is nothing that we cannot accomplish—this includes being the proud parent that God has called us to be. We must trust God to give us Godly wisdom on how to be Godly parents. There will be battles, and there will be tests, but God assures us in His Word that He is with us wherever we go. We can overcome any obstacle or opposition that is before us with God's help. We can do "all things" with His help. When we commit all to God and love Him with everything we have—our body, soul, and spirit—God will definitely work it out for our good, giving us the courage and strength to endure. Yes, He will!

Yes, there were challenges from time to time in raising these four beautiful gifts from God. There were many times when it took all I had to hang in there, especially when there were four teenagers in my house at one time. Their needs went from little needs to big needs. It takes a lot out of you when you are trying to make sure all their needs are met, besides your own needs. But, I can honestly say I feel so blessed that they never got out of control to the point where I lost hope and wanted to give up on my faith in God or in them.

During my tests and struggles that I faced on this assignment from God, I depended heavily on His Word, fellowship with other believers, and prayer to get me through. It was my faith and hope in God that helped me remain strong, praying constantly for strength and wisdom, day and night. Through it all, I learned how to trust in Jesus, and I learned how to depend and trust in God. I grew from "faith to faith".

Truly, I am mightily grateful to God for His grace and mercy. God helped me and made my burdens lighter as I surrendered ALL to Him and trusted Him to see me through every situation. Therefore, I give God all the glory, honor, and praise because without His help, I know beyond a shadow of a doubt that I could not have done this on my own. I have truly witnessed God's awesomeness during my single-parenting journey, and I want to encourage you that with God, "nothing is impossible" (Luke 1:37).

I truly love God. He continues to be faithful to His Word. Through the many obstacles I faced, I never gave up on God, and He never gave up on me. Hallelujah! I never stopped trusting. I never stopped reading and believing His Word. I never stopped praying. I never stopped expecting His best for my family. I still believe that the best is yet to come. When you get discouraged along the way, read and mediate on God's Word, day and night, for "good success". Make Joshua 1:8-9 a personal confession, and be successfully blessed. Make up your mind and be determined that with God's help, you can do this. You, too, can be a proud parent when you seek God's help...for there is "nothing too hard for the Lord" (Jeremiah 32:17, 27).

Chapter 20

Grown And Gone

Praise ye the Lord: praise him in the firmament of his power.
—Psalm 150:1

Praise and glory to God! My children are grown and gone. They have all grown up to be well-rounded, productive young adults—holding their own. They are all Christians. It was sort of frightening when they all left home to go their separate ways— college, marriage, and to do their own thing. When they had all finally left—Tracie was the last one to leave for college—I felt lost. I asked God, "What am I going to do now?" My life had been consumed with them in everything. I was in shock for a while because I was used to doing everything for and with them. One of my sisters encouraged me to go on and do some of the things I wanted to do in life. So I tried moving on to the next chapter of my life. I went back to school and earned several degrees. I spent a lot of time reading, traveling, conducting spiritual workshops and seminars. I also finished my secular work career, and God blessed me to retire in dignity.

I am so grateful to God for His grace and mercy, and for His divine favor and help along the way. His "rod and staff" (Psalm 23:4) did comfort and encourage me. He was with me all the time, through good times and bad times, and I never stopped praising and thanking Him, no matter how it looked. I know today that we were walking "by faith and not by sight" (2 Corinthians 4:7). Had we been walking by sight alone, we probably would have fainted or given up along the way. Thank God for endurance. I kept the faith, and I fought a good fight of faith. God is faithful. (1 Thessalonians 5:24: Faithful is he that calleth you, who also will do it.) Thank God for His great faithfulness.

Love God completely. Love your children entirely. One day they will be grown and gone. You will miss them terribly, but you will also be filled with joy knowing they have made you a proud parent. We still are very close in communication, whether on our own conference prayer line, texts, phone calls, visits, or even on Facebook. Staying in close communication is very important whether you are near or far. We cherish our close-knit relationship.

Chapter 21

Some Of Their Successes

O give thanks unto the Lord: for he is good:
for his mercy endureth forever.
—Psalm 136:1

Hard work, determination, and perseverance really do pay off. Today, I look back at the sacrifices that were made and the time spent in raising my children, and it makes me feel very proud. I know God is proud also. These are some of their accomplishments.

Sonya completed an Associate of Science (AS) from Tallahassee Community College (TCC) in Computer Technology, and an Associate of Arts (AA) from TCC. She is enrolled in a social work program at Florida A & M University. One of her goals is to become a counselor for young girls. Sonya has also earned a Bachelor of Arts in Ministry from Revelation Message Bible College. She has been involved in church ministries, including the praise team dance ministry and leadership ministry. Sonya worked for and retired from state government.

Corey is a licensed minister at his local congregation. He completed his bachelor degree in criminal justice from Morris Brown College in Atlanta, Georgia. He has earned two master's degrees from Central Michigan University: one in leadership and one in adult education. Corey also has his own business. He is the CEO of Vision, Pursuit, and Destination, LLC, a motivational-speaking company. Corey is an accomplished author. His book, *I Thought About Success...I Am Success* inspires many---adults, youths, and business leaders.

Adrienne completed a degree program at Jacksonville Community College as a paralegal. She later changed her career goals to become a registered nurse; she completed the nursing program and she is now a traveling nurse. Adrienne attends church regularly wherever she is located and maintains her affiliation with her home church. She is currently pursuing an advanced degree as a nurse practitioner. Adrienne has a lot of compassion for the sick and the dying. I often remind her that her career is not only a job but it is also a ministry, and she agrees.

Tracie attended Florida Memorial University with a major in elementary education and a minor in music. Teaching and singing are her gifts and passions. When it comes to the arts, she is very creative and skillful. Tracie's anointed gift in music has enabled her to extensively travel throughout the United States. She beautifully sings several types of music. Tracie sings in her local church choir, and she also sings at different community functions. She aspires to do her own CD album in the future.

I sincerely give thanks to the LORD for blessing my family. The many challenges, trying moments, and loving and firm discipline have really paid off. I thank God for it all, and to Him I give all the glory, the honor, and the praise. How grateful I am to God for blessing me with my children and helping me raise them the best that I knew how. I thank God for sending us the necessary assistance and help along the way. God is so awesome!

Chapter 22

Some Parenting Practices That Helped Me As A Single Parent

And they said, Believe on the Lord Jesus Christ,
and thou shalt be saved, and thy house.
—Acts 16:31

Here are some of the things that I practiced while raising my children alone. I believe they will be a blessing to you also.

(1) Be visible. **Visit the children's school. Get to know their teachers, the principal, and anyone who will come in contact with your children. Know their friends. Their classmates and teachers will respect you simply for the fact that you show love for your children, especially when you visit their school. Always be a concerned parent. When possible, be involved in the school's activities—PTOs and special events sponsored by the school. Also, get involved in the church's activities that your children participate in. It may not appear to be so, but your children feel very special when you show up and take part in their activities. We always attended church together. I was very visible, and my children appreciated it. Monday was my day off**

from work, and I would go to my children's school almost every Monday. Their teachers and their classmates knew me well.

(2) Be concerned about their health. **Make sure that you get your children the necessary medical attention—a physical at least once a year. If there is a health issue, attend to it immediately. Fortunately, my children were healthy and did not have to be in and out of the doctor's office. I think I had one emergency room ordeal—a broken ankle. Of course, I had my own home remedies. I used to give them a teaspoon of Father John every morning. It had minerals in it that I believed helped their immune system stay healthy and strong. I do not even know today how it tastes, but they would take it every morning faithfully without frowning. One thing I do know is that it helped keep them well, along with the spinach and the beets. They also took the Flintstones vitamins once a day.**

Make sure that their dental needs are met. Dental health is very important. I would take my children to the dentist every six months for a dental checkup. They never had cavities while they were young; they all had beautiful teeth. I scheduled my appointment at the same time as I did theirs; however, I did not always keep my appointment. I wish I had because I am doing major dental work right now that seems to be costing me a fortune. While you take care of your children's physical needs, be sure to take care of your own needs. I never baked any sweets while they were young. I told them that sweets were bad for their teeth. My mother would always have a baked cake, and that's where we ate the home-made sweets.

(3) Be willing to make the necessary sacrifices that it takes. **Put God first on your agenda in everything you do and ask Him for His divine guidance and direction. Ask God for**

wisdom and trust Him to give it to you. James 1:5 says, "If any of you lack wisdom, let him ask of God that giveth to all men liberally and upbraideth not; and it shall be given him."

It does not mean that you have to stop living or stop enjoying your life when you make sacrifices for your children. In reality, it means that a part of your life has just begun---to see their lives unfold right before you, to watch them grow up. It's so amazing! It will, however, mean that you will not have the privilege of just thinking about "me" or doing all the things you would do if there were no children. It means that you just have to do things that they could be a part of the majority of the time. Always keep your priorities in order.

I tried to involve my children in almost everything that I did. This is because I decided up front that these were my treasures that God had given to me, and I would do whatever it took to make sure they had a good life as best as I could. I realized that I was responsible for them and they were my priority next to God. When I was singing in a gospel group, I would always take them with me, all four of them. Sometimes on Sunday nights, we would get home late, and they had to go to school the next day. They really enjoyed going, and they all developed an interest in music, especially singing. We even had us a little singing group together. We all took piano lessons together.

Finally, I gave up the adult singing group. I really enjoyed singing, but I had to think of what was best for my children at that time. I thought being out late on the weekend would eventually interfere with their schooling, and I wanted them to get enough rest. So I joined the church choir, and it did not involve going out and coming in late at night. We could all leave and come in together at a reasonable hour. That worked out just fine for us.

I always tried to be involved in activities that my children could be a part of because I just did not trust my children with anyone. I had a real bad experience with a baby sitter when they were really young and, it caused me to never want to leave them alone with anyone unless it was urgently necessary. Briefly, I had a lady keeping them. I didn't know in the beginning that she was an alcoholic. She hid that habit very well until one day I came to pick up my children and received some very disturbing news. Sonya said that Corey was rolling Adrienne around like she was a ball. I asked where the babysitter was. Sonya said she had gone to the store. It was later that I found out what store she had gone to—a liquor store—and left my children unattended. Of course, I found a new babysitter—Mrs. Allen who has gone on to be with the Lord. She took excellent care of my children as if they were her own. From that point on, unless it was an emergency, I kept my own children. My life was not boring because I was doing what I wanted to do—taking care of my children and making sure they were safe. Use your own discretion when leaving your children with someone. Be careful who you leave them with, including relatives.

(4) Treat your children with respect. **Know their individual personality and treat them accordingly. This comes by spending quality time with them, listening to them and watching their actions, reactions, and interactions. Yes, it may be hard after coming in from an exhausting day's work or school, but you must find time to interact with your children—a must! Of course, there are different personalities that you must interact with differently, but the love must be the same for all of them.**

(5) Show love all the time, even when discipline has to take place. **They may not appreciate it now, but later in life, they will understand and even thank you for it. When they become adults, they will admit that you should have been harder on them—my children do now. You must show**

love—show them that you love them all equally. Hug your children every day if you have the opportunity to do so, and tell them you love them every time you see them or communicate with them. Compliment them: tell them that they are beautiful, intelligent, and smart. Encourage them and love on them every chance that you get.

(6)   No favoritism. **I never showed favoritism. If you would ask my children together or separately who is Mama's favorite, (as stated earlier) they would all tell you, "Mama loves all of us the same." There is a story in the Bible (Genesis) of Esau and Jacob. It demonstrated how their parents showed favoritism in their family, and it caused a lot of chaos. It caused the family to be extremely dysfunctional. Even though I had to deal with different personalities, and some required a little more attention than others, I respected and loved them the same. I never detected any jealousy among them, then or now. Although Corey was the only male in the house, he still did not get any more special attention than the girls. They were all treated fairly. Today, Corey may get a lot of attention from his sisters because they are so proud of him and his accomplishments.**

(7)   Build your children up. **Show them tender affection. Be the first to tell them that you love them, that you're proud of them, that they will be great and successful. So when someone else comes along with impure motives and tell them those things, they have already heard it from you. Encourage them verbally—this will help build their self-esteem and self-confidence. Even though they may be young, they share some of the same oppositions and struggles that we face. They just do not know how to express them, or they may be afraid to express them. They**

are your children—love on them! I do it even today, and my children are grown. They are still my babies forever.

(8)   Teach them God's Word. **Spend time in the Word with them. Deuteronomy 6:6-7: "And these words, which I command thee this day, shall be in thine heart: And thou shalt teach them unto thy children, and shalt talk of them when thou sitteth in thine house, and when thou walketh by the way, and when thou lieth down, and when thou riseth up." The amount of time and whatever works best for your family is entirely up to you. The main thing is to teach them God's Word. Answer their questions when they have some, and be honest with them when you do not have the answer at the moment. Let them know you will research the answer and get back with them as soon as possible. Honesty is very important.**

(9)   Spend time alone with God, in the Word, and in prayer. **As a parent, this is urgent. I spent many nights alone with God when the children were asleep. I have to be honest, I did shed many tears also. Looking back, I sought every means of help from the Lord—intimate time, prayer time, and Word study time. The prayers that I received from Life Study Fellowship (LSF) encouraged me, along with my own personal and private devotion. LSF had prayers for every situation, and anytime something came up that I needed assistance from the Lord and someone to agree with me, I requested that prayer topic. Below is one particular prayer that I prayed for God to help me raise my family alone. There were others that pertained to my family's needs, but this one really touched my heart and mind—I prayed, I believed, and I received. This is the prayer that I would like to share with you:**

Prayer for God's Help in Raising My Family

Train up a child in the way he should go, and
when he is old, he will not depart from it.
—Proverbs 22:6

Loving, Heavenly Father, creator of every living thing, now is the time I pray to Thee in this home Thou hast given us and in which Thou hast blessed me with a dear, good family.

Thou knowest all about us, dear Father, so I do not need to tell Thee all the trials I often have in raising my family. Thou knowest how tired and worn-out I get just trying to look out for them, and how they sometimes worry me. They are dear, good children, Father, but sometimes their words and actions are not what I would like. Thou understandest, Father.

Help me to be a good parent, dear Father, and raise my family right. Help me always to remember what I know in my heart, that whether small or grown-up, they will always be just my babies. Help me do this, and I know I can understand and help them. Teach me this, and I know I can keep them good and honest and pure.

O Father, I know Thou hearest my prayer, I know Thou will love and protect and guide me and my family and help me raise them so we shall all be one lovely, happy family of Thine.

In the name of Jesus, who took little children up His arms and said, "Suffer the little children to come unto me . . . for of such is the Kingdom of Heaven." Amen. (Life Study Fellowship)

My prayer life and my time in fellowship with God really helped me to endure tough times. I learned as much as I could about the subject of prayer. I used the Holy Bible as my main resource on prayer, and I also have many books on prayer that I purchased on the subject. These resources encouraged me on the power of prayer as well as how to pray for my children, my children's future, and their lives in general. I still have some of the books and prayers after all these years.

When my children were asleep, I would anoint their foreheads in the form of a cross with olive oil and pray over them. (They called it the Jesus oil.) I called their names and asked God to bless them in every area of their lives, to protect them that they would have Godly friendships and mates; that they would be successful in school and in their future careers; that they would be kind, loving, and obedient. There were other concerns that I had for them, and I prayed for those as they occurred. Sometimes I prayed throughout the day for certain matters. I still pray for my children daily and throughout the day. After giving thanks to God for a new day, I pray Psalms 91 and the Prayer of Jabez (I Chronicles 4:10) over them faithfully for blessings and protection, as well as heartfelt prayers.

Today, when we are together in person, we pray together— never departing without having prayer. This prayer life is still a must in our lives. We take prayer and communication so seriously that one of my daughters set up a prayer conference call line for us. We pray together Monday through Friday, between 7:00 a.m. and 7:30 p.m. Sometimes, when the five of us are on the line, we go over thirty minutes. On those days, it's amazing how God arranges it that we all are available to talk longer than usual. When we have special concerns, such as family matters, job issues, medical appointments, relationship issues, etc., we call one another and come into agreement for victory in the situation. I send them daily prayer scriptures and encouragement during the week via text messages. Since we are located in different areas, it is so necessary for us to connect as much as possible and keep the communication and the love flowing all the time, and we do in one form or another.

(10) Keep them involved in positive activities. **My children stayed active in positive activities—-Boy Scouts and Girl Scouts. I was a Cookie Mom (um-m). They sang in community choirs and in their school chorales. Going to concerts and football games was very entertaining and exciting to me. I tried to keep them involved in as many positive activities and environments that I could, and I stayed involved in their activities as well. If they had a fund-raiser, I took part in it. Keeping them involved is very important.**

(11) Set aside quality time for your children. **Have a family night. Usually, Friday night was our family night. We would do a drive-in movie or have a crab night at home. The children enjoyed the drive-in movies because they could sit on the hood of the car and watch the movie. On crab nights, I would stop by the store and get them on the way home from work, and we had a ball eating them. Those were fun days, and I do miss them.**

We got plenty of devotional time together. I taught Sunday school, moving from teaching primary to high school teen classes. Each time my children got promoted in Sunday school, I would move to the next level with them. It was very interesting to see how they grew up physically and spiritually.

(12) Never belittle or degrade your children. **I cannot stress this enough. I have been in the grocery store and have heard some parents cursing, screaming at, and belittling their little ones. It really hurt me deeply. Do not call your children ugly or negative names. Even if they are not acting like angels, call them angels anyway. This is what you want them to be—angels, not devils. Like the word of God says, you have what you say (paraphrased—Mark 11:23). Speak over their lives only what you want them to be or become. I know it may seem hard in the beginning**

when they misbehave sometimes, but the more you do it, the easier it will become. "Faith cometh by hearing . . ." (Romans 10:17). They will begin to think they are angels after hearing it so much.

Sometimes my children would do some things that I did not agree with, and at some point, the devil would even try to make me hate my children for some of their mischievous actions, but I would say, "Devil, you will not make me hate my children. My children belong to Jesus! (I would even call their individual names.) God, you said, according to Acts 16:31, that my whole household would be saved, and I am claiming that promise in the name of Jesus." I would confess this over and over. I refused to belittle or degrade my children, and I refused to give up on them. Today, I still pray that prayer because I have grandchildren and great-grandchildren. Their future and their salvation are very important to me.

(13) Treasure your greatest investment—**Your children are your most precious possessions. They are your princes and princesses. Treat them as such. God has entrusted you with them. Don't disappoint God, them, or yourself. Every opportunity that I had, I encouraged my children to keep God first and to strive for greatness. Even today I still encourage them.**

(14) Use every moment as a teachable moment. **I am emphasizing this because I believe it is very important. Do not discipline or punish your children without teaching them the reason behind it. Let them learn from each mistake and each accomplishment. You are your child's best teacher.**

(15) Be open and honest about questions or topics that they ask you. **You would rather for them to hear from you what is right or wrong than to hear it from the world. With the**

social media and technology that our children have access to today, it is best that parents talk to them first. If we do not address their concerns and answer their questions, the media and the world surely will. Therefore, be open about topics such as dating, drugs, sex, and anything else that they may inquire about.

(16) Lead by example. **Live a moral Godly life of integrity before your children. Model good behavior. Of course, we are not perfect beings, but there is a certain level of respect that we owe to our children. If we make a mistake before them, be willing to apologize and teach them the importance of admitting an error and correcting it.**

(17) Pray for your children daily. **Always intercede for your children: that God's plan for their lives to be fulfilled; that they will be free from drugs, alcohol, rebellion, accidents, and disease. Pray that they increase in wisdom and in favor with God and man. Pray that they will be sexually pure until they are married. Pray that the gifts that God has given them will be used to the glory of God. Pray that they will be healthy and successful, that they will have Godly friendships and Godly mates. Pray that they will be free from unhealthy habits and unhealthy relationships. Pray that they will be saved at an early age and that their hearts and minds will be open to the leading and guidance of the Holy Spirt. Pray that they will be protected from the evils of this world. Even if they are adults now, still pray for them. I do.**

(18) Take time for yourself. **I am adding this even though I cannot testify that I did it as much as I should have. I was, as my children say, overly protective of them, and since I did not trust anyone with my children, I did not do much "me" time. I am suggesting that you take some**

time out for yourself. This is the one thing that I would do differently if I had to start all over again as a single parent. I would take a little more time for myself. Try to find someone you can trust to keep your children, even if it is only for a short period of time. I enjoyed raising them, and I enjoyed being with them, however, I could have had more balance in my life. I realized that if you do not make some time for yourself, it could have some kind of effect on you later in life. My quiet time was usually when I dropped them off at the skating rink, or perhaps maybe a movie. Do find a way to take time out for yourself. Balance in your life is very necessary.

Chapter 23

Scriptures And Confessions For Parents

Isaiah 54:13 – All thy children shall be taught of the Lord; and great shall be the peace of thy children.

CONFESSION: My children shall be taught of the Lord, and they will have the peace of God.

Psalm 112:1–2 – Praise ye the LORD: Blessed is the man that feareth the LORD, that delighteth greatly in his commandments. His seed shall be mighty upon the earth, and they shall be blessed forever.

CONFESSION: I fear God; I delight in His commandments. My children shall be mighty upon the earth, and they shall be blessed of God forever.

Psalm 115:14 – The Lord shall increase you more and more: you and your children.

CONFESSION: God shall continually bless me and my children in abundance.

Psalm 127:3 – Lo, children are a heritage of the LORD; and the fruit of the womb is his reward.

CONFESSION: My children are God's gifts to me, and I thank God for them.

Proverbs 22:6 – Train up a child in the way he should go: and when he is old, he will not depart from it.

CONFESSION: I will loving instruct my children in the path of the Lord and in the way of righteousness in obedience to God's Word.

Exodus 20:12 – Honor thy father and thy mother: that thy days may be long upon the land which the LORD thy God giveth thee.

CONFESSION: My children will obey God's commandments to respect their parents so that they may have a long life with satisfaction.

Ephesians 6:1–4 – Children obey your parents in the Lord, for this is right. Honor your father and mother which is the first commandment with promise. That it may be well with thee, and thou mayest live long upon the earth. And ye fathers, provoke not your children to wrath: but bring them up in the nurture and admonition of the Lord.

CONFESSION: My children will be obedient to their parents for this is the right thing to do in the sight of God, and I will not provoke my children to anger.

Acts 16:31 – And they said, Believe on the Lord Jesus Christ, and thou shall be saved, and thy house.

CONFESSION: I believe **on the Lord Jesus Christ; I am saved and my whole household is saved.**

(Call their names in these confessions.)

Proverbs 29:17 – Correct thy son, and he shall give thee rest; yea, he shall give delight unto thy soul.

CONFESSION: My children will receive necessary correction and discipline from me so that they will bring joy to my soul.

Proverbs 23:13 – Withhold not correction from the child: for if thou beatest him with the rod, he shall not die.

CONFESSION: I will chasten and discipline my children when necessary and they will have a long and prosperous life.

Proverbs 23:24 – The father of the righteous shall greatly rejoice; and he that begetteth a wise child shall have joy of him.

CONFESSION: I will guide my children in the wisdom of God, and they will bring me joy.

Proverbs 17:6 – Children's children are the crown of old men: and the glory of children are their fathers.

CONFESSION: My children and my grandchildren are my crowns and my gifts from God; I thank Him for them.

I Peter 5:7 – Casting all thy care upon him, for he careth for you.

CONFESSION: I cast all my cares and concerns upon God, trusting Him in all things, because He cares for my children and me.

Psalm 91:11 – For he shall give his angels charge over thee, to keep thee in all thy ways.

CONFESSION: God encamps angels around my children and me, and they keep us safe in all our ways.

Psalm 3:3 – But thou, O Lord, art a shield for me, my glory, and the lifter up of mine head.

CONFESSION: When times seem to be a little rough, I look to God to cover us with His love and keep our heads lifted up high.

Matthew 21:22 – And all things whatsoever ye shall ask in prayer, believing, ye shall receive.

CONFESSION: I will spend time praying over my children that all their needs are met, and I believe and receive God's best for them.

John 14:13-14 – And whatsoever ye shall ask in my name, that will I do, that the Father may be glorified in the Son. If ye shall ask any thing in my name, I will do it.

CONFESSION: In the name of Jesus, I thank God that my children are saved and no weapon formed against them shall prosper.

Isaiah 55:12 – For ye shall go out with joy, and be led forth with peace: the mountains and the hills shall break forth before you into singing, and all the trees of the field shall clap their hands.

CONFESSION: God will guide me in joy and peace as I do my best in raising my children whom He has entrusted me with.

Isaiah 65:23 – They shall not labor in vain nor bring forth for trouble; for they are the seed of the blessed of the Lord, and their offspring with them.

CONFESSION: I am encouraged by God that my labor in raising my children is not in vain, and we are the blessed of the Lord.

I John 3:22 – And whatsoever we ask, we receive of him, because we keep his commandments, and do those things that are pleasing in his sight.

CONFESSION: I believe in the power of prayer that God will answer my prayers for my children as I continue to be obedient to His Word and live a righteous life.

Psalm 91:1-2 – He that dwelleth in the secret place of the Most High shall abide under the shadow of the Almighty. I will say of the Lord, He is my refuge, my fortress, my God, in him will I trust.

CONFESSION: I will dwell in the secret place of the Most High and teach my children to do so because God is our protection and our shelter, and my trust is in Him.

Isaiah 43:2 – When thou passeth through the waters, I will be with thee; and through the rivers they shall not overflow thee: when thou walketh through the fire, thou shalt not be burned, neither shall the flame kindle upon thee.

CONFESSION: No matter what comes in our pathway, God is with us, and He will not let us to be moved because He is always with us to protect us.

Isaiah 54:17 – No weapon formed against thee shall prosper, and every tongue that shall rise against thee in judgment, thou shalt condemn: for this is the heritage of the servants of the Lord, and their righteousness is of me, saith the Lord.

CONFESSION: Any evil thing that forms itself against my children and me will not prosper, and every tongue that rises against us in judgment shall be condemned. We are protected because we are God's servants and our righteousness is of God.

Psalm 91:9-10 – Because thou hast made the Lord which is thy refuge, even the Most High thy habitation. There shall no evil befall thee, neither shall any plague come nigh thy dwelling.

CONFESSION: God will keep me and my children sheltered from evil and harm because He is our shield.

Psalm 17:8 – Keep me as the apple of thy eye; hide me under the shadow of thy wings.

CONFESSION: God will cover my children and me, and He will protect and love us at all times.

Proverbs 20:20 – Whoso curseth his father or his mother, his lamp shall be put out in obscure darkness.

CONFESSION: I will teach my children to obey the Word of God concerning honor, obedience, and respect to their parents so that they will have a long and satisfied life.

Colossians 3:20 – Children, obey your parents in all things: for this is well pleasing unto the Lord.

CONFESSION: I will teach my children that God is pleased when they obey and honor their parents.

Proverbs 1:8–9 – My son, hear the instruction of thy father, and forsake not the law of thy mother: For they shall be an ornament of grace unto thy head, and chains about thy neck.

CONFESSION: I will teach my children to be obedient to their parents, for God will be pleased, and He will bless their obedience.

Galatians 6:9 – And let us not be weary in well doing: for in due season we shall reap, if we faint not.

CONFESSION: I will not grow weary in "well doing" for my children, for God will greatly reward me for my faithfulness and sacrifices.

1 Corinthians 10:31 – Whether therefore ye eat, or drink, or whatsoever ye do, do all to the glory of God.

CONFESSION: Everything I do in raising my children, and for my children after they are grown, I will do it to the glory of God.

Proverbs 3:5–6 – Trust in the Lord with all thine heart; and lean not unto thine own understanding. In all thy ways acknowledge him, and he shall direct thy path.

CONFESSION: I will trust in the Lord with my whole heart, and I will acknowledge Him and trust Him to order and direct my paths and instruct my children to do the same.

Proverbs 2:1–5 – My son, if thou will receive my words, and hide my commandments with thee; So that thou incline thine ear unto wisdom, and apply thine heart to understanding; Yea, if thou crieth after knowledge, and liftest up thy voice for understanding; If thou seeketh her as silver, and searchest for her as for hid treasures; Then shalt thou understand the fear of the Lord, and find the knowledge of God.

CONFESSION: I will always seek God for wisdom in all my undertakings so that every decision I make concerning my life and the life of my children will be a wise decision.

Deuteronomy 6:6-7 -- And these words, which I command thee this day, shall be in thine heart; And thou shalt teach them unto thy children, and shalt talk of them when thou sitteth in thine house and when thou walketh by the way, and when thou liest down, and when thou risest up.

CONFESSON: I will obey the commandments of the Lord and I will be faithful to teach them to my children so that they will have blessed lives.

Mark 11:24 – And what things soever ye desire, when ye pray, believe that ye receive them, and ye shall have them.

CONFESSION: I believe that I receive whatever I pray for as I pray for the things that God has willed in His Word for my children and me.

And if it seems evil unto you to serve the Lord, choose you this day whom ye will serve; whether the gods which your father served that were on the other side of the flood, or the gods of the Amorites, in whose land ye dwell: but as for me and my house, we will serve the LORD.

CONFESSION: As for me and my house, we will serve the Lord. Amen.

John 3:16 – For God so loved the world, that He gave His only begotten Son, that whosoever believeth in Him should not perish, but have everlasting life.

Chapter 24

Prayers For Children And Parents

Prayer for Children

Dear Heavenly Father, I come to You in the precious name of our Lord and Savior Jesus Christ. I thank You for blessing me with my children. I realize that they are gifts from You. Father, I pray that You will bless my children's lives abundantly, above and beyond anything that they can ask or imagine. Make them the men and women of God that You have created them to be.

I pray for their salvation, that they will be sensitive to the leading of the Holy Spirit. Fill them with an abundant overflow of Your spirit. Forever bless their lives with divine health and divine prosperity. As I teach them Your Word, I pray that they will observe and obey Your Word. Help them trust and depend on Your guidance at all times. Protect them from all evil and harm and cover them with the blood of Jesus.

I pray that they will have Godly mates, healthy relationships, healthy habits, a blessed and great future. I thank you, Father, because you are the Most High God, and with you all these things are possible. Thank you, Lord God, for hearing and answering my prayer. To you, Father, be all the glory and all the honor and all the praise. In Jesus' name, I believe and receive these blessings for my children. Amen.

Prayer for Parents

Heavenly Father, in the name of Jesus, I come to You, thanking You and praising You for all Your blessings. You are a great God who is excellent in all Your ways. Father, I pray that You will make me the parent that You have created me to be from the foundation of the world.

Bless me to be sensitive to the leading of the Holy Spirit as I face the challenges of parenting. Help me make wise decisions when it comes to being a good parent. Help me to make Godly decisions concerning the welfare of my children. Whatever task that is set before me, please help me undertake it lovingly with all my heart as unto You.

Show me how to teach my children in the ways of righteousness through Your Word, and let me always model excellent behavior before them. When it comes to disciplining and counseling my children, I pray that I will do it firmly but lovingly.

I thank You for helping me be a good and proud parent, and I praise You in advance for all these blessings. In Jesus' holy and righteous name, I pray. To God be the glory! Amen.

Chapter 25

Testimonials From Single Parents

I am a God-fearing single mother. Does that make being a single mother easier? No. Surrendering my life to Jesus has given me much wisdom, understanding, and strength to be a single mother. Have I not made mistakes and fumbled along the way? Yes. I am so thankful for a forgiving God. Being a single mother is a big responsibility on one person. You need all the help, positive help, you can get. You need good advice and encouragement. You have the responsibilities that two parents would have.

The more I grew spiritually, the more I took my job as a single mother more responsibly and seriously. I thought, "God, these are my beautiful children, and I am their mother. It is my job to watch over them and protect them. The Lord is going to hold me accountable for my children." So I started on my job watching over them, teaching them the Word of God, praying over them every day, and living my life as an example for them in the home and outside of the home. We would never leave home without prayer. I strongly believe in prayer. I knew I could not be with them twenty-four hours a day, but God could.

I knew I had to work, and I had to make sure my children were in a safe environment. I needed childcare. Before I would place my children in childcare, I would visit different facilities and talk to other single mothers about childcare facilities. I refused to place my children at a daycare facility where I did not feel comfortable with. When my children were of school age, I would get as much information as possible for the best schools for them. Education is very important to me. I would be very involved with their schools and activities.

As much as possible, my children and I would have devotion time and family time. We would play games together. We attended church regularly, and I kept my children involved in church activities and some sport activities.

Single mothers, I share this with you. I could not have done my job as a single mother if I had not put God first in my life. You nurture, you teach your children what is right and what is wrong. They might not always make the right decisions, and when they do not make the right decisions, it is good to know Jesus. I assure you, from my experience, when you need help, direction, strength, and wisdom, you talk to Jesus for whatsoever help or decision you need. He will be there for you. When you are alone, as a single parent, as a single mother, you need a friend like Jesus!

Be blessed.

Belinda Miller

Can a woman teach her kids to have good manners? Of course, you can. As a single mom, I was able to successfully raise my two sons. They both have graduated from high school and enlisted in the US Marines Corps after graduation. Both have completed five years of military service. They are enrolled in college and working part time. This path that they chose was based on their interest in continuing to learn the values of life, to develop their own self-discipline, as well as to further their education.

As far as manners are concerned, this was something that was taught from their early beginning years. I have always felt that kids who learn good manners would learn self-respect and respect for others, particularly for older people. This is something that is so lacking in the world today.

Our children need guidance and direction. If we, as parents, do not teach them right from wrong, they will observe and learn from the world around them. I say this because there is nothing as nice as seeing a young man with good manners.

Many times I have been complimented on how well I raised my sons, but the greatest joy of it all is whenever I hear it from them: "Mom, we really appreciate you." That's when I would reflect to one of my favorite scriptures that I have always believed in—Proverbs 22:6: "Train up a child in the way he should go, and when he is old he will not depart from it."

Blessings and love,

Valarie Paulino

Chapter 26

Parents' Thought-Provoking Questionnaire

(Mainly for young parents, but optional to all)
(Comments/optional, use a separate paper/pad, if necessary)

What were your first thoughts of being a single parent?

_____
_____
_____
_____
_____

How much quality time do you spend with your children?

_____
_____
_____
_____
_____

Do you plan and monitor their activities?

_____
_____
_____
_____
_____

**What kind of disciplinary measures do you use?
Are there any you would consider changing?**

_____
_____
_____
_____
_____

Do you attend parent/teacher conferences and PTO's?

_____
_____
_____
_____
_____

Do you know your children's teachers?

_____
_____
_____
_____
_____

Do your children have a spiritual/prayer life?

_____
_____
_____
_____
_____

**Do you teach them the importance of good
manners and being respectful?**

_____
_____
_____
_____
_____

Do you try, with all your heart, to meet their basic needs?

_____
_____
_____
_____
_____

Do you know their friends?

_____
_____
_____
_____
_____

Do you love and respect your children?

_____
_____
_____
_____
_____

Do you hug your children?

_____
_____
_____
_____
_____

Do you tell your children that you love them daily?

_____
_____
_____
_____
_____

Do you help them with their homework and review it with them?

_____

_____

_____

_____

_____

Do you teach your children to respect themselves, others, and others' property?

_____

_____

_____

_____

_____

Do you teach them the importance of obedience?

_____

_____

_____

_____

_____

Do you show/teach your children how to love?

_____

_____

_____

_____

_____

Do you teach your children the importance of getting along with others?

_____
_____
_____
_____
_____

Do you play favorites?

_____
_____
_____
_____

Do you talk with your children about drugs, peer pressure, and sex (unhealthy relationships/unhealthy habits)?

_____
_____
_____
_____

What other things do you and your children talk about?

_____
_____
_____
_____

Do you still trust God when parenting hurts?

_____
_____
_____
_____

Is it your ultimate goal to be a proud and successful parent?

_____

_____

_____

_____

_____

Closing Remarks

Jeremiah 29:11 says, "For I know the thoughts that I think toward you, saith the LORD, thoughts of peace, and not of evil, to give you an expected end."

God is gracious in all His ways. The plans that He has for our lives, He will fulfill.

At one point, I thought I would never get my children out of diapers. Look at them now—God-fearing, loving, kind, mature, and super ambitious individuals. They are all grown-up and have gone their separate ways. Just witnessing the grace and the mercy of God in my life firsthand in helping me raise my children, it teaches me to continue to hold on to His unchanging hand. He is not finished with me yet because he has blessed me to be a "big grandmother" and a "big great-grandmother," along with many spiritual daughters and sons.

Truly glory, honor, and praise belong to God for magnifying Himself in my life and in the lives of my children. It amazes me every time I am in their presence and observe how God continues to bless and mature them. Thanks be to God who has enabled me to remain *"steadfast, unmoveable, always abounding in the work of the Lord."* I consider raising my children as a part of His work in my life. He has shown me and continues to show me that *"my labor is not in vain in the Lord"* (*1 Corinthians 15:58*).

I feel so proud and I also feel that I am one of the most blessed and successful mothers in the whole wide world. My children made me a proud parent. *Single Parents Can Be Proud Parents---My Story to His Glory*. To God be the glory!

"Father, I thank you for your abounding grace, for helping me to raise my children to honor and reverence you, and to be honorable and respectful individuals. I thank you, O God, that they have made me a proud parent in so many ways, and that they are making you proud also. I truly love them and they truly love me, and I appreciate you for loaning them to me. I pray your continued blessings in every area of our lives. Thank you, Father, for every person that has been called to this single-parenting ministry, and to the ministry of parenting as a whole. Please bless every single parent to be a proud parent. Bless every parent to be a proud parent. Give them the courage, direction, endurance, and the wisdom that they need to fulfill this calling. I pray that all the plans that you have ordained for their lives will come to pass. Thank you, Father, and thank you Sonya, Corey, Adrienne, and Tracie. In Jesus's name. Amen."

Notes

The Holy Spirit

Life Study Fellowship – "With God All Things
Are Possible" – A Handbook of Life. Copyright
1944, 1972 by Life Study Fellowship

King James Version
(Authorized Version). First published in
1611. Quoted from the KJV Classic
Reference Bible, Copyright 1983 by
The Zondervan Corporation.

KJV Old Testament Hebrew Lexicon...Bible Hub - Lexixon.
www.biblehub.com

THE HOLY BIBLE, NEW INTERNATIONAL
VERSION, Copyright 1973, 1978, 1984, 2011 by
Biblica, Inc. Used by permission.

"Single Mother Statistics" https://singlemotherguide.com

About the Author

Dr. Juanita Shaw is a Spirit-filled minister of God who loves God, His Word, and His people. She is the proud mother of four loving children, a "big" grandmother, and a "big" great-grandmother-- the loves of her life.

Dr. Shaw is a graduate of Booker T. Washington High School, Miami, Florida; Broward Community College (Associate of Arts), Fort Lauderdale, Florida; Florida A & M University (Bachelor of Social Work), Tallahassee, Florida; and, Jacksonville Theological Seminary (Bachelor of Arts in Biblical Studies, Master of Arts in Christian Education, and Doctor of Theology), Jacksonville, Florida.

In her retirement, she spends her time traveling and volunteering in the community. She has received several awards and recognitions for outstanding community service, including the Living Legend Community Service Award from her high school alma mater (National Alumni Association/Foundation), and the Barack Obama Presidential Lifetime Achievement Award for community service.

Dr. Shaw has traveled extensively throughout many states ministering the Gospel in Word and song, as well as conducting spiritual seminars and workshops. Her ultimate desire is to be a blessing to others and to fulfill the call of God on her life.

CONTACT INFORMATION:
DR. JUANITA SHAW
jtshaw46@gmail.com

XLIBRIS